MW01206032

Dr. John Chung's

AMC 10, 12 PREP.

Second Edition

No Material

Preface

Dr. John Chung has taught American Mathematics Competitions (AMC) for 20 years to many students. When he first taught, he tried to explain the process systematically. Students still had many difficulties mastering the concepts because there was no organized book on the topic. Dr. Chung wanted to create a system for students to master the concepts of AMC more comfortably. Dr. Chung wrote this book specifically to meet students' needs and take an organized approach to learning that students could easily grasp.

This book is designed to help students learn the most fundamental topics easily and make AMC accessible through exercises and past exam questions. Students can develop their foundational skills with this book, and then build up that foundation to master advanced mathematical skills to solve problems themselves.

"I want this book to give you confidence in AMC. I hope you always have an inquiring mind and look forward to a bright and fantastic future. Thank you."

- Dr. John Chung

No Material

Contents

#	Topics	Page #
1	Positive divisors (Factors) using Prime Factorization	7
2	Ratio of the Area of two Triangles with same Height	10
3	Triangle after two isosceles triangles built in right triangle is a right triangle	13
4	Right Triangle Proportion	14
5	Concurrent (Angle Bisector, Median, Altitude, Perpendicular Bisector)	16
6	Cyclic Quadrilaterals	19
7	Stewart's Theorem	24
8	Ptolemy's Theorem	26
9	Circle	29
10	Tangent Spheres	38
11	Similar Figures	39
12	How to find the inner point?	42
13	How to find the length which divides sides into $a:b$?	43
14	Inclination of parallel lines	45
15	Trace by a disk around a Square	47
16	Polygon	49
17	Graphs of $|x|+|y|=c$ and $|x|-|y|=c$	51
18	Identical Equation	53
19	Average Speed	54
20	Relative Speed	55
21	Algebra with Integer solutions (Special Equations)	56
22	Absolute Value Equation	59
23	Discriminant	60
24	Simplifying Complex Radical	61
25	Sum of Digits of a Number	62
26	How to solve $ax+by=c$	63
27	Vieta's Formulas	65
28	LCM and GCF(GCD)	68
29	Modular Arithmetic	70
30	Sequence and series	75
31	Counting Techniques	77

#	Topics	Page #
32	Dividing People into Groups	79
33	Counting multiples of a number	81
34	How to find the largest n such that 2^n divides 100!?	83
35	Stars and Bars	85
36	How to distribute distinct things into different rooms	87
37	Pigeonhole Principle	89
38	How many squares does contain diagonal?	91
39	How to check if a number is prime	93
40	Base Number	94
41	Decimal Base Number	96
42	Divisibility Rules	98
43	Number of Subsets	100
44	Greatest Integer Function	101
45	Greatest Integer Equation	103
46	Transformation of Greatest Integer Equation	105
47	General Probability	106
48	Geometric Probability	107
49	Symmetric Probability (1)	108
50	Symmetric Probability (2)	110
51	Logarithm	111
52	Factoring $x^{2n+1}+1$, $x^{2n+1}-1$	113
53	Express a number as sum of consecutive positive numbers	115
54	Abraham de Moivre's Formula	117
55	Roots of $f(x)=x^n-1$	120
	Answers and Explanations	

If n is a positive integer with prime factorization, and
$$n = p_1{}^{n_1} \cdot p_2{}^{n_2} \cdot p_3{}^{n_3} \cdots p_k{}^{n_k},$$
then the number of factors is $(n_1 + 1)(n_2 + 1)(n_3 + 1) \cdots (n_k + 1)$

Example 1: Find the number of factors (positive divisors) of 12600.

Solution) $12600 = 2^3 \cdot 3^2 \cdot 5^2 \cdot 7^1$

Number of factors $= (3+1)(2+1)(2+1)(1+1) = 72$

Factors of 2^3	Factors of 3^2	Factors of 5^2	Factors of 7^1
$2^0 = 1$	$3^0 = 1$	$5^0 = 1$	$7^0 = 1$
2^1	3^1	5^1	7
2^2	3^2	5^2	
2^3			
Number of Positive Divisors is $(3+1)(2+1)(2+1)(1+1) = 72$			

Example 2: Find the number of positive even divisors of 12,600.

Solution) We know that even $\times$ any natural number = even.

Factors of 2^3	Factors of 3^2	Factors of 5^2	Factors of 7^1
$2^0 = 1$	$3^0 = 1$	$5^0 = 1$	$7^0 = 1$
$\left[2^1\right]$	3^1	5^1	7
$\left[2^2\right]$	3^2	5^2	
$\left[2^3\right]$			
Number of Positive Even Divisors is $3 \times 3 \times 3 \times 2 = 54$			

Example 3: How many of positive divisors are odd?

Solution) We know that $odd \times odd \times odd \cdots = odd$

From the table above, the number of positive odd divisors is
$1 \times 3 \times 3 \times 2 = 18$.

Sum of all Positive Divisors of 12 with prime factorization $2^2 \times 3^1$ is

$S = \left(2^0 + 2^1 + 2^2\right)\left(3^0 + 3^1\right) = 28$,

because $\left(2^0 + 2^1 + 2^2\right)\left(3^0 + 3^1\right) = 1 + 2 + 3 + 4 + 6 + 12$.

Example 4: What is the sum of all positive divisors of 12,600?

Solution) $12600 = 2^3 \cdot 3^2 \cdot 5^2 \cdot 7^1$

Sum of all positive divisors is

$\left(2^0 + 2^1 + 2^2 + 2^3\right)\left(3^0 + 3^1 + 3^2\right)\left(5^0 + 5^1 + 5^2\right)\left(7^0 + 7^1\right) = 48,360$

Product of all positive divisors of 12 with prime factorization $2^2 \times 3^1$:

Number of positive divisors is $(2+1)(1+1) = 6$.

$\left(1 \times 12\right)\left(2 \times 6\right)\left(3 \times 4\right) = 12^{6/2} = 12^3$

Example 5: What is the product of all positive divisors of 120?

Solution) $120 = 2^3 \times 3^1 \times 5^1 \quad \rightarrow \quad$ Number of Factors $= (3+1)(1+1)(1+1) = 16$

Product is $120^{16/2} = 120^8$

PRACTICE

1. How many positive integer divisors of 51^6 are perfect squares?

   A) 15   B) 16   C) 20   D) 25   E) 27

2. How many positive integer divisors of 51^6 are perfect cubes?

   A) 5   B) 6   C) 9   D) 12   E) 15

3. How many positive integer divisors of 51^6 are perfect squares or perfect cubes?

  A) 21   B) 25   C) 27   D) 30   E) 35

4. How many positive integer divisors of 201^9 are perfect squares or perfect cubes (or both)? (2019 AMC 10A #11)

  A) 32   B) 36   C) 37   D) 39   E) 41

5. How many positive integer divisors does 201^9 have?

6. What is the product of the positive integer divisors of 21^3?

7. What is the sum of all positive integer divisors of 21^3?

8. When you choose a number from all positive integer divisors of 12600, what is the probability the number is even?

9. For each positive integer n, let $f_1(n)$ be twice the number of positive integer divisors of n, and for $j \geq 2$, let $f_j(n) = f_1(f_{j-1}(n))$. For how many values of $n \leq 50$ is $f_{50}(n) = 12$? (2021 AMC 10A #23, AMC 12A #21)

  (A) 7   (B) 8   (C) 9   (D) 10   (E) 11

2	Ratio of the Area of two Triangles with same Height

The ratio of areas of two triangles with the same height is equal to the ratio of their bases.

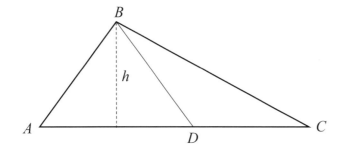

If A_1 = Area of $\triangle ABD$ and A_2 = Area of $\triangle BCD$, Then $\dfrac{A_1}{A_2} = \dfrac{AD}{DC}$.

Proof:

$$A_1 = \frac{AD \times h}{2} \text{ and } A_2 = \frac{DC \times h}{2}$$

Therefore, $A_1 : A_2 = \dfrac{AD \times h}{2} : \dfrac{DC \times h}{2} = AD : DC.$ → $\dfrac{A_1}{A_2} = \dfrac{AD}{DC}$

PRACTICE

1. Point E is the midpoint of side $\overline{CD}$ in square $ABCD$, and $\overline{BE}$ meets diagonal $\overline{AC}$ at F. The area of quadrilateral $AFED$ is 45. What is the area of $ABCD$? (2018 AMC)

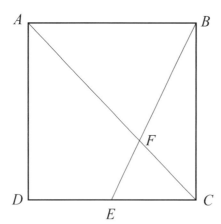

(A) 100   (B) 108   (C) 120   (D) 135   (E) 144

2. Point E intersects side $\overline{DC}$ in rectangle $ABCD$ and $\overline{BE}$ meets diagonal $\overline{AC}$ at F. If the area of quadrilateral $ADEF$ is 66 and $\dfrac{DE}{EC} = 2,$ what is the area of $\triangle EFC$?

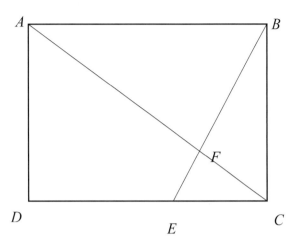

(A) 6   (B) 8   (C) 9   (D) 10   (E) 12

3. In triangle ABC, point D divides side $\overline{AC}$ so that $AD:DC = 1:2.$ Let E be the midpoint of $\overline{BD}$ and F be the point of intersection of line $\overline{BC}$ and line $\overline{AE}$. Given that the area of $\triangle ABC$ is 360, what is the area of $\triangle EBF$? (2019 AMC)

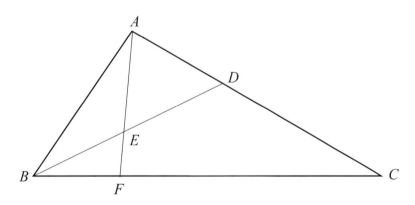

(A) 24   (B) 30   (C) 32   (D) 36   (E) 380

4. In triangle ABC, point D divides side $\overline{AC}$ so that $AD:DC = 1:3$. Let E be the midpoint of $\overline{BD}$ and F be the point of intersection of line $\overline{BC}$ and line $\overline{AE}$. Given that the area of $\triangle ABC$ is 80, what is the area of $\triangle EBF$?

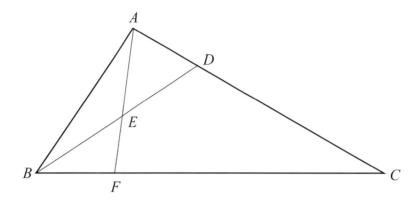

(A) 2   (B) 3   (C) 4   (D) 6   (E) 7

3	Triangle after two isosceles triangles built in right triangle is a right triangle

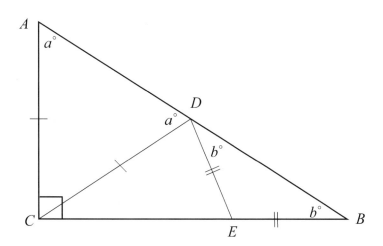

If $\triangle ACD$ and $\triangle BDE$ are isosceles with $AC = CD$ and $DE = EB$ respectively, then, $\triangle CDE$ is a right triangle.

Since $a + b = 90°, \angle CDE = 180 - (a + b) = 90$.

PRACTICE

1. In $\triangle ABC$ with a right angle at C, point D lies in the interior of $\overline{AB}$ and point E in the interior of $\overline{BC}$ so that $AC = CD$, $DE = EB = 5$. and the ratio $AC:DE = 4:3$. What is the ratio $AD:DB$? (2019 AMC 10B #16)

(A) 2:3   (B) $2:\sqrt{5}$ (C) 1:1   (D) $3:\sqrt{5}$ (E) 3:2

2. In $\triangle ABC$ with a right angle at C, point D lies in the interior of $\overline{AB}$ and point E in the interior of $\overline{BC}$ so that $AC = CD = 12$, $DE = EB = 5$. What is the area of $\triangle CDE$?

(A) 20   (B) 24   (C) 30   (D) 36   (E) 60

3. In $\triangle ABC$ with a right angle at C, point D lies in the interior of $\overline{AB}$ and point E in the interior of $\overline{BC}$ so that $AC = CD = 15$, $DE = EB = 8$. What is the area of $\triangle DEB$?

(A) 24   (B) $\dfrac{480}{17}$ (C) 32   (D) 36   (E) 60

When we draw an altitude to the hypotenuse of a right triangle, we create two new triangles with especially important properties as follows.

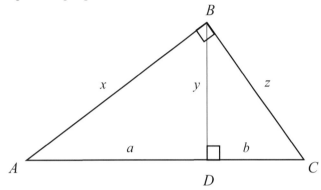

1. $x^2 = a(a+b)$ 2. $y^2 = ab$ 3. $z^2 = b(b+a)$ 4. $\dfrac{xz}{2} = \dfrac{(a+b)y}{2}$

Prove $y^2 = ab$: Method 1 using similar

Since $\triangle ABD \sim \triangle BDC,$ $\dfrac{y}{a} = \dfrac{b}{y}.$ $\rightarrow y^2 = ab$

Prove $y^2 = ab$: Method 1 using a circle.

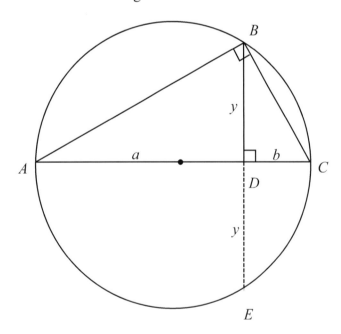

Since $\angle B = 90°$, $\overline{AC}$ is a diameter and $DE = BD = y$.

Therefore, $y \cdot y = a \cdot b \rightarrow y^2 = ab$.

Prove $x^2 = a(a+b)$ using a circle. Since $\angle BDC = 90°$, $\overline{BC}$ is the diameter of the circle.

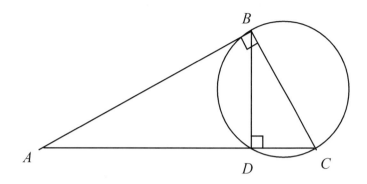

By definition, $AB^2 = AD \cdot AC \rightarrow x^2 = a(a+b)$

PRACTICE

1. Given a triangle with side lengths 15, 20, and 25, find the triangle's smallest height.

   (2002 AMC 10A #13)

   (A) 6   (B) 12   (C) 12.5   (D) 13   (E) 15

2. Use the figure and given information, find the length of $\overline{AC}$, $\overline{BC}$, and $\overline{CD}$.

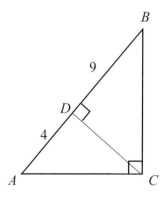

3. Quadrilateral ABCD satisfies $\angle ABC = \angle ACD = 90°$, $AC = 20$, and $CD = 30$. Diagonals $\overline{AC}$ and $\overline{BD}$ intersect at point E and $AE = 5$. What is the area of Quadrilateral $ABCD$? (2020 AMC 12A #18)

   (A) 330   (B) 340   (C) 350   (D) 360   (E) 370

<table>
<tr><td>**5**</td><td>Concurrent (Angle Bisector, Median, Altitude, Perpendicular Bisector)</td></tr>
</table>

In a triangle, three lines which pass through the same point are **concurrent.**

A. Angle bisectors are concurrent.

An angle bisector is the line which passes through the vertex of an angle and divides the angle into two equal angles.

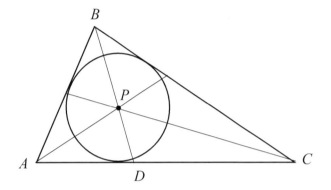

1) Point P is the incenter.   2) There is an inscribed circle.

3) $\dfrac{AB}{BC} = \dfrac{AD}{DC}$

B. Medians are concurrent.

Median is the line drawn from a vertex to the midpoint of the opposite side.

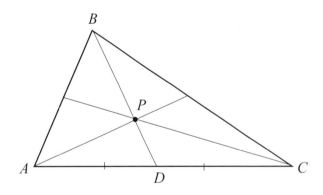

1) Point P is the centroid.   2) The centroid divides each median in the ratio of $2:1$.

3) $\dfrac{BP}{PD} = \dfrac{2}{1}$

C. Orthocenters are concurrent.

Altitude is the perpendicular line drawn from a vertex to the opposite side.

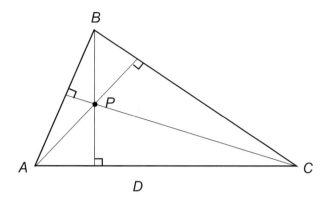

    1) Point P is the orthocenter.

D. Perpendicular bisectors are concurrent.

Perpendicular bisector is the line which is perpendicular to a segment and passes through the midpoint of the segment.

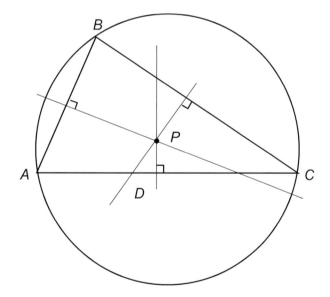

    1) Point P is the circumcenter.
    2) There is a circumscribed circle.

PRACTICE

1. Nondegenerate $\triangle ABC$ has integer side lengths, $\overline{BD}$ is an angle bisector, $AD = 3$, and $DC = 8$. What is the smallest possible value of the perimeter? (2010 AMC 10A #16)

   (A) 30   (B) 33   (C) 35   (D) 36   (E) 37

2. Triangle ABC with $AB = 50$ and $AC = 10$ has area 120. Let D be the midpoint of $\overline{AB}$, and let E be the midpoint of $\overline{AC}$. The angle bisector of $\angle BAC$ intersects $\overline{DE}$ and $\overline{BC}$ at F and G, respectively. What is the area of quadrilateral $FDBG$?
   (2018 AMC 18A #24, AMC 12A #23)

   (A) 60   (B) 65   (C) 70   (D) 75   (E) 80

6	Cyclic Quadrilaterals

A. If a quadrilateral inscribed in a circle, then the quadrilateral is a cyclic quadrilateral.

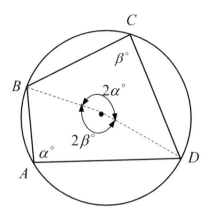

We know that the inscribed angle is half of the central angle for the same arc and

$$2(\alpha + \beta) = 360 \quad \rightarrow \quad \alpha + \beta = 180$$

Formula: The sum of the opposite angles in a cyclic quadrilateral is $180°$.

$$\angle A + \angle B = 180° \quad \text{and} \quad \angle B + \angle D = 180°$$

Note: Square, rectangle, and isosceles trapezoid are cyclic.

B. In the figure, If $\angle ABD = \angle ACD$, quadrilateral $ABCD$ is cyclic.

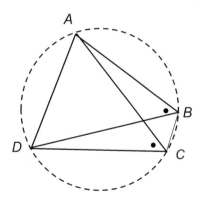

C. In the figure, if $(AE)(EC)=(DE)(EB),$ quadrilateral $ABCD$ is cyclic

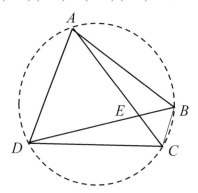

Example 1: In the diagram below, if $\angle ABD = 55°$ and $\angle ADE = \angle ACB,$ what is the
measure of $\angle ACD$?

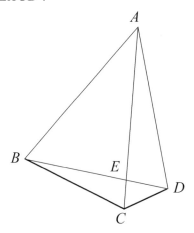

Solution) From $m\angle ADE = m\angle ACB,$ we can see quadrilateral $ABCD$ is cyclic.
    Inscribed angles for the same arc AD are equal in measures.
    $m\angle ABD = m\angle ACD = 55°$

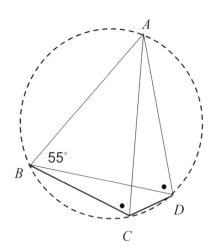

PRACTICE

1. In the figure, P is the center of the circle. If $m\angle BPD = 100°$ and $m\angle CBD = 15°$, what is the measure of $\angle BDC$?

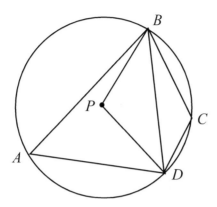

2. If $AP = 3$, $BP = 6$, $CP = 8$, $DP = 4$, and $\angle ABP = 40°$, what is the measure of $\angle PCD$?

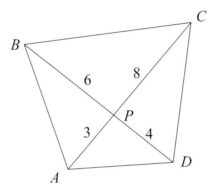

3. In the figure, $ABCD$ is cyclic quadrilateral whose diagonals intersect at point P such that $m\angle DBC = 50°$ and $m\angle BAC = 60°$. What is $m\angle BCD$?

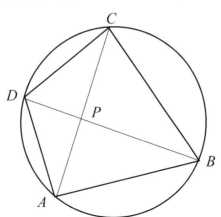

4. In the given figure, point P is the orthocenter of $\triangle ABC$. If $\angle BAE = 30°$ and $\angle DCA = 20°$, what is the measure of $\angle EDC$?

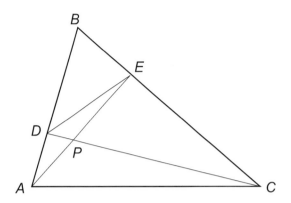

5. Let $ABCD$ be a parallelogram with area 15. Points P and Q are the projections of A and C, respectively, onto the line BD, and points R and S are the projections of B and D, respectively, onto the line AC. See the figure, which also shows the relative locations of these points.

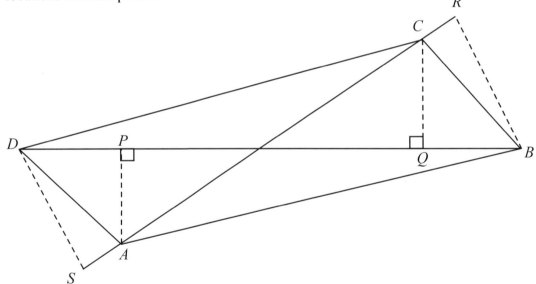

Suppose $PQ = 6$ and $RS = 8$, and let d denote the length of $\overline{BD}$, the longer diagonal of $ABCD$. Then d^2 can be written in the form $m + n\sqrt{p}$, where $m, n,$ and p are positive integers and p is not divisible by the square of any prime. What is $m + n + p$?
(2021 AMC 12B #24)

(A) 81   (B) 89   (C) 97   (D) 72   (E) 85

22

6. Isosceles triangle ABC has $AB = AC = 3\sqrt{6}$, and a circle with radius $5\sqrt{2}$ is tangent to line AB at B and to line AC at C. What is the area of the circle that passes through vertices A, B, and C? (2021 AMC 10A #15)

(A) 24π (B) 25π (C) 26π (D) 27π (E) 28π

7	Stewart's Theorem

The theorem can be proved as an application of the law of cosines. Let θ_1 be the angle between $\overline{AD}$ and $\overline{BD}$ and θ_2 the angle between $\overline{BD}$ and $\overline{DC}$. Then θ_2 is the supplement of θ_1, and so $\cos\theta_2 = -\cos\theta$. Applying the law of cosines in the two small triangles using angles θ_1 and θ_2 produces

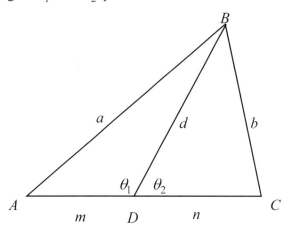

Let $AB = a$, $BC = b$, $BD = d$, $AD = m$, and $DC = n$. By the law of cosine,

$$a^2 = m^2 + d^2 - 2md\cos\theta_1$$
$$b^2 = n^2 + d^2 - 2nd\cos\theta_2$$

$\rightarrow$

$$a^2 = m^2 + d^2 - 2md\cos\theta_1 \quad \cdots\cdots(1)$$
$$b^2 = n^2 + d^2 + 2nd\cos\theta_1 \quad \cdots\cdots(2)$$

From $(1)n+(2)m$,

$$a^2n = m^2n + d^2n - 2mnd\cos\theta_1 \quad \cdots\cdots(1)$$
$$b^2m = n^2m + d^2m + 2mnd\cos\theta_1 \quad \cdots\cdots(2)$$

$\rightarrow \quad a^2n + b^2m = mn(m+n) + d^2(m+n)$

Therefore, the equation of Stewart's theorem is

$$a^2n + b^2m = \left(d^2 + mn\right)(m+n)$$

PRACTICE

1. Triangle ABC has $AB = 13$, $BC = 14$ and $AC = 15$. Let P be the point on $\overline{AC}$ such that $PC = 10$. There are exactly two points D and E on line BP such that Quadrilaterals $ABCD$ and $ABCE$ are trapezoids. What is the distance DE? (2021 AMC 12B #11)

(A) $\dfrac{42}{5}$ (B) $6\sqrt{2}$ (C) $\dfrac{84}{5}$ (D) $12\sqrt{2}$ (E) 18

2. In $\triangle ABC$, $AB = 86$, and $AC = 97$. A circle with center A and radius AB intersects $\overline{BC}$ at points B and X. Moreover $\overline{BX}$ and $\overline{CX}$ have integer lengths. What is BC?
(2013 AMC 12A #19)

(A) 11   (B) 28   (C) 33   (D) 61   (E) 72

3. In $\triangle ABC$, we have $AB = 1$ and $AC = 2$. Side $\overline{BC}$ and the median from A to $\overline{BC}$ have the same length. What is BC? (2002 AMC 12B #23)

(A) $\dfrac{1+\sqrt{2}}{2}$ (B) $\dfrac{1+\sqrt{3}}{2}$ (C) $\sqrt{2}$ (D) $\dfrac{3}{2}$ (E) $\sqrt{3}$

In Euclidean geometry, Ptolemy's theorem is a relation between the four sides and two diagonals of a cyclic quadrilateral (a quadrilateral whose vertices lie on a common circle)

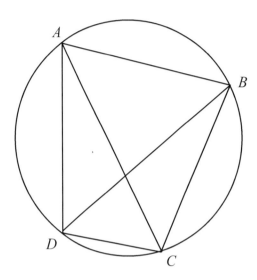

In the figure above, $AB \cdot CD + BC \cdot AD = AC \cdot BD$

Proof

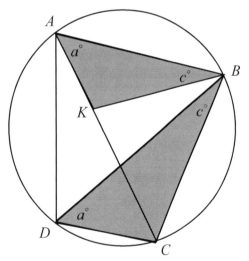

Figure 1

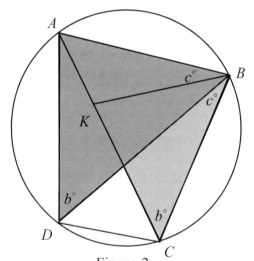

Figure 2

Let $ABCD$ be a cyclic quadrilateral. On the chord BC, the inscribed angles $\angle BAC = \angle BDC = c°$. Construct K on AC such that $\angle ABK = \angle CBD$ and $\angle CBK = \angle ABD$.

Now, by common angles $\triangle ABK$ is similar to $\triangle DBC$, and likewise $\triangle ABD$ is similar to $\triangle KBC$. Thus,

In figure 1, $\dfrac{AK}{AB} = \dfrac{CD}{BD} \rightarrow AK \cdot BD = AB \cdot CD$ ......(1).

In figure 2, $\dfrac{CK}{BC} = \dfrac{AD}{BD} \rightarrow CK \cdot BD = AD \cdot BC \quad \cdots\cdots(2)$

From $(1)+(2)$

$$AK \cdot BD + CK \cdot BD = AB \cdot CD + AD \cdot BC \rightarrow (AK + CK)BD = AB \cdot CD + AD \cdot BC$$

And $AK + CK = AC.$ Therefore,

$$AC \cdot BD = AB \cdot CD + AD \cdot BC$$

Special case:

Equilateral triangle ABC with a side s: $AC = s$, $AD = p$, $BD = r$, and $CD = q$

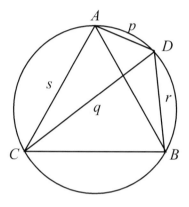

From Ptolemy's theorem, $qs = ps + rs \rightarrow q = p + r$

PRACTICE

1. In the figure, $ABCD$ is a quadrilateral with diagonals AC and BD intersecting at E. If $BE = 4$, $DE = 6$, $AE = 8$, $CE = 3$, and $AB = 6$, what is AD?

   (A) 12   (B) $\sqrt{166}$ (C) 13   (D) $2\sqrt{83}$ (E) 15

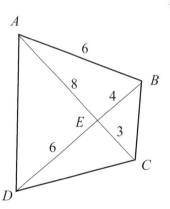

2. In triangle ABC we have $AB = 7$, $AC = 8$, $BC = 9$. Point D is on the circumscribed circle of the triangle so that AD bisects angle BAC. What is the value of $\dfrac{AD}{CD}$? (2004 AMC 10 #24)

   (A) $\dfrac{9}{8}$ (B) $\dfrac{5}{3}$ (C) 2   (D) $\dfrac{17}{7}$ (E) $\dfrac{5}{2}$

3. Let $\triangle ABC$ be an equilateral triangle. Let P be a point on minor arc AB of its circumcircle. Which of the following is true?

(A) $PC > PA + PB$ (B) $PC = PA + PB$ (C) $PC < PA + PB$

(D) $PC = \dfrac{PA + PB}{2}$ (E) $PC = PA \cdot PB$

4. A hexagon is inscribed in a circle. Five of the sides have length 81 and the sixth, denoted by $\overline{AB}$, has length 31. Find the sum of the lengths of the three diagonals that can be drawn from A. (1991 AIME #14)

9	Circle

To crash the circle questions, use the <u>centers</u> and the <u>properties</u> of a triangle (especially right triangle).

PRACTICE

1. A circle centered at O has radius 1 and contains the point A. The segment AB is tangent to the circle at A and $\angle AOB = \theta$. If point C lies on $\overline{OA}$ and $\overline{BC}$ bisects $\angle ABO$, then $OC =$ (2000 AMC 12 #17)

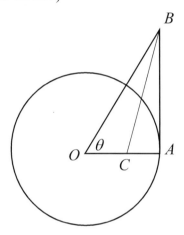

(A) $\sec^2 \theta - \tan \theta$ (B) $\dfrac{1}{2}$ (C) $\dfrac{\cos^2 \theta}{1 + \sin \theta}$ (D) $\dfrac{1}{1 + \sin \theta}$ (E) $\dfrac{\sin \theta}{\cos^2 \theta}$

2. A circle centered at A with a radius of 1 and a circle centered at B with a radius of 4 are externally tangent. A third circle is tangent to the first two and to one of their common external tangents as shown. The radius of the third circle is (2001 AMC 12 #18)

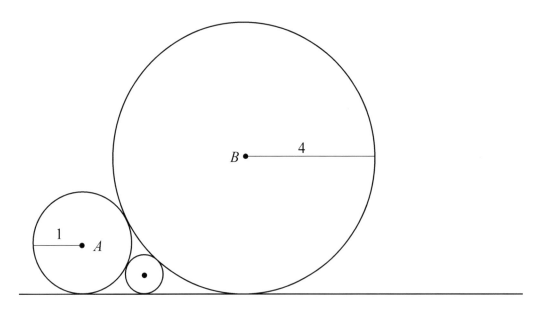

(A) $\dfrac{1}{3}$ (B) $\dfrac{2}{5}$ (C) $\dfrac{5}{12}$ (D) $\dfrac{4}{9}$ (E) $\dfrac{1}{2}$

3. Let C_1 and C_2 be circles defined by

$$(x-10)^2 + y^2 = 36 \text{ and } (x+15)^2 + y^2 = 81$$

respectively. What is the length of the shortest line segment PQ that is tangent to C_1 at P and to C_2 at Q? (2002 AMC 12A #18)

(A) 15 (B) 18 (C) 20 (D) 21 (E) 24

4. Each of the small circles in the figure has radius one. The innermost circle is tangent to the six circles that surround it, and each of those circles is tangent to the large circle and to its small-circle neighbors. Find the area of the shaded region. (2002 AMC 12 #5)

(A) π (B) 1.5π (C) 2π (D) 3π (E) 3.5π

5. Square $ABCD$ has sides of length 4, and M is the midpoint of $\overline{CD}$. A circle with radius 2 and center M intersects a circle with radius 4 and center A at points P and D. What is the distance from P to $\overline{AD}$? (2003 AMC 12A #17)

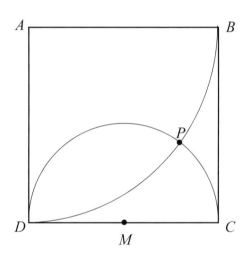

(A) 3   (B) $\dfrac{16}{5}$ (C) $\dfrac{13}{4}$ (D) $2\sqrt{3}$ (E) $\dfrac{7}{2}$

6. A, B and C are externally tangent to each other, and internally tangent to circle D. Circles B and C are congruent. Circle A has radius 1 and passes through the center of D. What is the radius of circle B? (2004 AMC 12 #19)

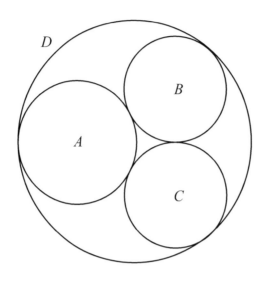

(A) $\dfrac{2}{3}$ (B) $\dfrac{\sqrt{3}}{2}$ (C) $\dfrac{7}{8}$ (D) $\dfrac{8}{9}$ (E) $\dfrac{1+\sqrt{3}}{3}$

7. Square $ABCD$ has side length 2. A semicircle with diameter $\overline{AB}$ is constructed inside the square, and the tangent to the semicircle from C intersects side $\overline{AD}$ at E. What is the length of $\overline{CE}$? (2004 AMC 12 #18)

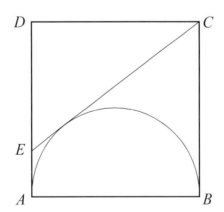

(A) $\dfrac{2+\sqrt{5}}{2}$ (B) $\sqrt{5}$ (C) $\sqrt{6}$ (D) $\dfrac{5}{2}$ (E) $5-\sqrt{5}$

8. An annulus is the region between two concentric circles. The concentric circles in the figure have radii b and c, with $b > c$. Let OX be a radius of the larger circle, let XZ be tangent to the smaller circle at Z, and let OY be the radius of the larger circle that contains Z. Let $a = XZ$, $d = YZ$, and $e = XY$. What is the area of the annulus? (2004 AMC 12B #10, AMC 10B #12)

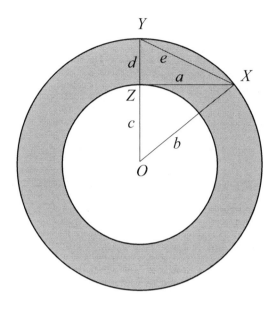

(A) πa^2 (B) πb^2 (C) πc^2 (D) πd^2 (E) πe^2

9. Let $\overline{AB}$ be a diameter of a circle and C be a point on $\overline{AB}$ with $2 \cdot AC = BC$.

Let D and E be points on the circle such that $\overline{DC} \perp AB$ and $\overline{DE}$ is a second diameter.

What is the ratio of the area of $\triangle DCE$ to the area of $\triangle ABD$? (2005 AMC 10A #23)

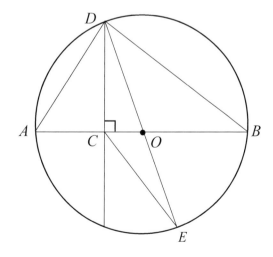

(A) $\dfrac{1}{6}$ (B) $\dfrac{1}{4}$ (C) $\dfrac{1}{3}$ (D) $\dfrac{1}{2}$ (E) $\dfrac{2}{3}$

10. Three circles of radius s are drawn in the first quadrant of the xy-plane. The first circle is tangent to both axes, the second is tangent to the first circle and the x-axis, and the third is tangent to the first circle and the y-axis. A circle of radius $r > s$ is tangent to both axes and to the second and third circles. What is $\dfrac{r}{s}$? (2005 AMC 12A #16)

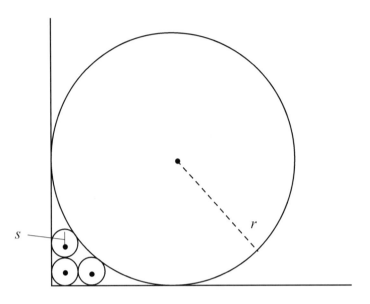

(A) 5　　　(B) 6　　　(C) 8　　　(D) 9　　　(E) 10

11. A circle of radius r is concentric with and outside a regular hexagon of side length 2. The probability that three entire sides of hexagon are visible from a randomly chosen point on the circle is $\dfrac{1}{2}$. What is r? (2006 AMC 12A #22)

(A) $2\sqrt{2} + 2\sqrt{3}$　　(B) $3\sqrt{3} + \sqrt{2}$　　(C) $2\sqrt{6} + \sqrt{3}$　　(D) $3\sqrt{2} + \sqrt{6}$　　(E) $6\sqrt{2} - \sqrt{3}$

12. Circles with centers $(2,4)$ and $(14,9)$ have radii 4 and 9, respectively. The equation of a common external tangent to the circles can be written in the form $y = mx + b$ with $m > 0$. What is b? (2006 AMC 12A # 19)

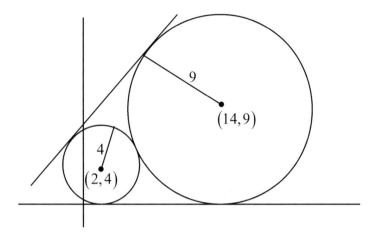

(A) $\dfrac{908}{119}$ (B) $\dfrac{909}{119}$ (C) $\dfrac{130}{17}$ (D) $\dfrac{911}{119}$ (E) $\dfrac{912}{119}$

13. A circle with center C is tangent to the positive x and y-axis and externally tangent to the circle centered at $(3,0)$ with radius 1. What is the sum of all possible radii of the circle with center C? (2009 AMC 12A #16)

(A) 3   (B) 4   (C) 6   (D) 8   (E) 9

14. For how many integer values of k do the graphs of $x^2 + y^2 = k^2$ and $xy = k$ not intersect? (2010 AMC 12A #13)

(A) 0   (B) 1   (C) 2   (D) 4   (E) 8

15. Circles with centers A and B have radii 3 and 8, respectively. A common internal tangent intersects the circles at C and D, respectively. Lines AB and CD intersect at E, and $AE = 5$. What is CD? (2006 AMC 12A #16, AMC 10 #23)

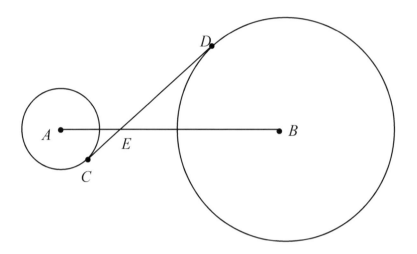

(A) 13　(B) $\dfrac{44}{3}$　(C) $\sqrt{221}$　(D) $\sqrt{255}$　(E) $\dfrac{55}{3}$

16. Which of the following describes the graph of the equation $(x+y)^2 = x^2 + y^2$?
(2006 AMC 12A #11, AMC 10A #11)

(A) the empty set　(B) one point　(C) two lines　(D) a circle　(E) the entire plane

17. Circles with centers O and P have radii 2 and 4, respectively, and are externally tangent. Points A and B are on the circle centered at O, and points C and D are on the circle centered at P, such that $\overline{AD}$ and $\overline{BC}$ are common external tangents to the circles. What is the area of hexagon $AOBCPD$? (2006 AMC 12B #15, AMC 10B #24)

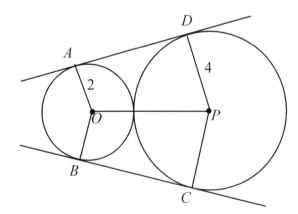

(A) $18\sqrt{3}$　(B) $24\sqrt{2}$　(C) 36　(D) $24\sqrt{3}$　(E) $32\sqrt{2}$

18. Two circles of radius 1 are to be constructed as follows. The center of circle A is chosen uniformly and at random from the line segment joining $(0,0)$ and $(2,0)$ The center of circle B is chosen uniformly and at random, and independently of the first choice, from the line segment joining $(0,1)$ to $(2,1)$. What is the probability that circles A and B intersect? (2008 AMC 12B #21)

(A) $\dfrac{2+\sqrt{2}}{4}$ (B) $\dfrac{3\sqrt{3}+2}{8}$ (C) $\dfrac{2\sqrt{2}-1}{2}$ (D) $\dfrac{2+\sqrt{3}}{4}$ (E) $\dfrac{4\sqrt{3}-3}{4}$

19. A circle of radius 1 is internally tangent to two circles of radius 2 at points A and B, where AB is a diameter of the smaller circle. What is the area of the region, shaded in the picture, that is outside the smaller circle and inside each of the two larger circles? (2004 AMC 10B #25)

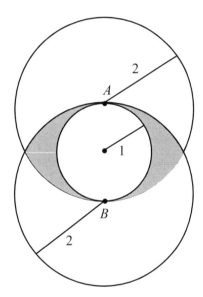

(A) $\dfrac{5}{3}\pi-3\sqrt{2}$ (B) $\dfrac{5}{3}\pi-2\sqrt{3}$ (C) $\dfrac{8}{3}\pi-3\sqrt{3}$ (D) $\dfrac{8}{3}\pi-3\sqrt{2}$ (E) $\dfrac{8}{3}\pi-2\sqrt{3}$

10	Tangent Spheres

1) Centroid of three tangent spheres with radius r

Point P is the centroid.

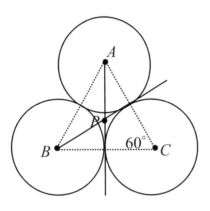

Remember: a) $\triangle ABC$ is an equilateral triangle.

b) The length of $BP = \dfrac{2r\sqrt{3}}{3}$

PRACTICE

1. Three pairwise- tangent spheres of radius 1 rest on a horizontal plane. A sphere of radius 2 rests on them. What is the distance from the plane to the top of the larger sphere? (2004 AMC 10A #25, 12A #22)

(A) $3 + \dfrac{\sqrt{30}}{2}$ (B) $3 + \dfrac{\sqrt{69}}{3}$ (C) $3 + \dfrac{\sqrt{123}}{4}$ (D) $\dfrac{52}{9}$ (E) $3 + 2\sqrt{2}$

2. Inside a right circular cone with base radius 5 and height 12 are three congruent spheres with radius r. Each sphere is tangent to the other two spheres, and also tangent to the base and side of the cone. What is r? (2021 AMC 10A #22)

(A) $\dfrac{3}{2}$ (B) $\dfrac{90 - 40\sqrt{3}}{11}$ (C) 2 (D) $\dfrac{144 - 25\sqrt{3}}{44}$ (E) $\dfrac{5}{2}$

11	Similar Figures

Two figures that have the same shape are said to be similar. When two figures are similar, their corresponding sides are in proportion.

Properties

1. If the ratio of the corresponding sides is $a:b$, the ratio of their areas is $a^2:b^2$, and the ratio of their volumes is $a^3:b^3$.
2. In similar triangles, the corresponding angles are equal in measure.

PRACTICE

1. Triangle ABC has $AB = 2 \cdot AC$. Let D and E be on $\overline{AB}$ and $\overline{BC}$, respectively, such that $\angle BAE = \angle ACD$. Let F be the intersection of segments AE and CD, and suppose that ΔCFE is equilateral. What is $\angle ACB$? (2010 AMC 10 A #14, 12A #8)

   (A) $60°$ (B) $75°$ (C) $90°$ (D) $105°$ (E) $120°$

2. A triangle with vertices $(6,5),(8,3)$, and $(9,1)$ is reflected about the line $x = 8$ to create a second triangle. What is the area of the union of the two triangles? (2013 AMC 10A #16)

   (A) 9 (B) $\dfrac{28}{3}$ (C) 10 (D) $\dfrac{31}{3}$ (E) $\dfrac{32}{3}$

3. In triangle ABC, $AB = 13$, $BC = 14$, and $CA = 15$. Distinct points D, E, and F lie on segments $\overline{BC}, \overline{CA}$, and $\overline{DE}$, respectively, such that $\overline{AD} \perp \overline{BC}$, $\overline{DE} \perp \overline{AC}$, and $\overline{AF} \perp \overline{BF}$. The length of segment $\overline{DF}$ can be written as $\dfrac{m}{n}$, where m and n are relatively prime positive integers. What is $m+n$? (2013 AMC 10 #23, 12B #19)

   (A) 18 (B) 21 (C) 24 (D) 27 (E) 30

4. All of the triangles in the diagram below are similar to isosceles triangle ABC in which $AB = AC$. Each of the 7 smallest triangles has area 1, and $\triangle ABC$ has area 40. What is the area of trapezoid $DBCE$? (2018 AMC 10A #9)

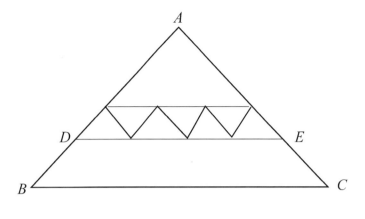

(A) 16   (B) 18   (C) 20   (D) 22   (E) 24

5. A paper triangle with sides of lengths 3, 4, and 5 inches, as shown, is folded so that point A falls on point B. What is the length in inches of the crease? (2018 AMC 10A #13)

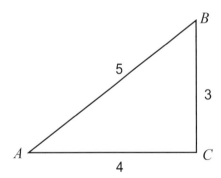

(A) $1 + \dfrac{\sqrt{2}}{2}$ (B) $\sqrt{3}$ (C) $\dfrac{7}{4}$ (D) $\dfrac{15}{8}$ (E) 2

6. Let $ABCD$ be a trapezoid with $\overline{AB} \parallel \overline{CD} \parallel \overline{EF}$, $AB = 7$, and $CD = 17$.
   If trapezoid $ABEF$ and $CDEF$ have the same area, what is the length of $\overline{EF}$?

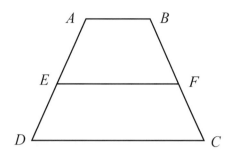

(A) 10　(B) 11　(C) 12　(D) 13　(E) 14

7. Trapezoid $ABCD$ has $\overline{AB} \parallel \overline{CD}$, $BC = CD = 43$, and $\overline{AD} \perp \overline{BD}$. Let O be the intersection of the diagonals $\overline{AC}$ and $\overline{BD}$, and let P be the midpoint of $\overline{BD}$. Given that $OP = 11$, the length of AD can be written in the form $m\sqrt{n}$, where m and n are positive integers and n is not divisible by the square of any prime. What is $m+n$? (2021 AMC 12A #17)

(A) 65　(B) 132　(C) 157　(D) 194　(E) 215

1) Midpoint of $A(x_1, y_1)$ and $B(x_2, y_2)$

$$M(x, y) = \left(\frac{x_1 + x_2}{2}, \frac{y_1 + y_2}{2} \right)$$

2) Point P such that divides the line segment $\overline{AB}$ in the ratio of $a:b$.

$$x = \frac{ax_2 + bx_1}{a+b}, \quad y = \frac{ay_2 + by_1}{a+b}$$

PRACTICE

1. What is the greatest integer less than or equal to $\dfrac{3^{100} + 2^{100}}{3^{96} + 2^{96}}$?

   (A) 80   (B) 81   (C) 96   (D) 97   (E) 625

2. The coordinates of the endpoints of $\overline{QS}$ are $Q(-9,8)$ and $S(9,-4)$. Point R is on $\overline{QS}$ such that $QR:RS$ is in the ratio of $1:2$. What are the coordinates of point R?

   (A) $(0,2)$ (B) $(-3,4)$ (C) $(3,0)$ (D) $(-6,6)$ (E) $(7,2)$

3. Which of the following intervals contain the value of $k = \dfrac{2^{302} + 3^{302}}{2^{300} + 3^{300}}$?

   (A) $0 < k < 2$ (B) $2 < k < 4$ (C) $4 < k < 6$ (D) $6 < k < 9$ (E) $9 < k < 12$

13	How to find the length which divides sides into ratio a:b?

Theorem 1

In the figure below, $\overline{AB} \parallel \overline{CD} \parallel \overline{EF}$ and $\overline{EF}$ divides $\overline{AD}$ and $\overline{BC}$ in the ratio $a:b$.
What is the length of $\overline{EF}$?

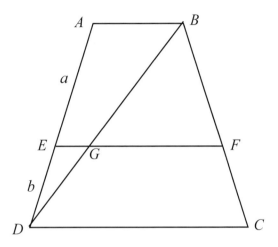

Since $EG = AB\left(\dfrac{b}{a+b}\right)$ and $GF = CD\left(\dfrac{a}{a+b}\right)$,

$$EF = EG + GF = \frac{a(CD) + b(AB)}{a+b} \ .$$

Theorem 2

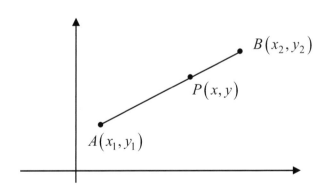

In the xy-plane, If $AP:BP = a:b$, then the coordinates of point P are

$$P\left(\frac{ax_2 + bx_1}{a+b}, \frac{ay_2 + by_1}{a+b}\right)$$

PRACTICE

1. Let $ABCD$ is a trapezoid with $\overline{AB} \parallel \overline{CD}$, $AB = 7$, and $CD = 17$. Point F and E are the midpoints of sides $\overline{AD}$ and $\overline{BC}$, respectively. What is the length of $\overline{FE}$?

   (A) 8   (B) 9   (C) 10   (D) 12   (E) 15

2. In the figure below, $BC = 6$ and $AD = 10$. If $\overline{BC} \parallel \overline{EF} \parallel \overline{AD}$ and $\dfrac{BE}{EA} = \dfrac{2}{5}$, then what is the length of $\overline{EF}$?

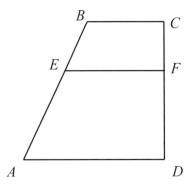

   (A) 7   (B) $\dfrac{50}{7}$ (C) $\dfrac{54}{7}$ (D) 8   (E) $\dfrac{57}{7}$

3. In the figure below, $AB = 6$, $CD = 12$, and $BC = 15$. If $\dfrac{AE}{ED} = \dfrac{3}{2}$, what is the area of $ABFE$?

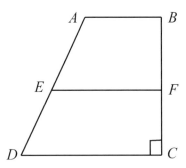

   (A) 68   (B) 69   (C) 70   (D) 70.2   (E) 72

44

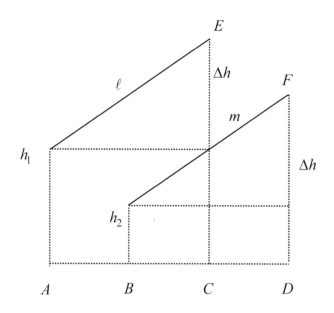

Theorem:

    If $AC = BD$ and lines ℓ and m are parallel, then their inclinations are equal.

    $EC = h_1 + \Delta h$ and $FD = h_2 + \Delta h$

Example:

If $AB = CD$ and $EF \parallel GH$, then $DH = CG + \Delta h = CG + (EF - BF)$

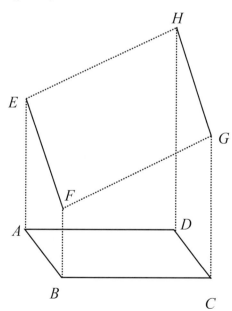

For $F(5)$, $E(9)$, and $G(13)$, $HD = G(13) + (9 - 5) = 14$.

PRACTICE

1. An architect is building a structure that will place vertical pillars at the vertices of regular hexagon $ABCDEF$, which is lying horizontally on the ground. The six pillars will hold up a flat solar panel that will not be parallel to the ground. The heights of pillars at A, B, and C are 12, 9, and 10 meters, respectively. What is the height, in meters, of the pillar at E?

   (2021 AMC 10A #17)

   (A) 9   (B) $6\sqrt{3}$ (C) $8\sqrt{3}$ (D) 17   (E) $12\sqrt{3}$

Trace by a disk around a square

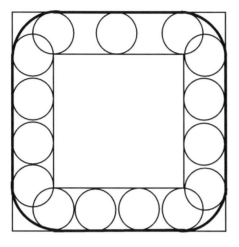

1. Trace by a disk of radius r around the outside of a square

1. Trace by a disk of radius r around the inside of a square

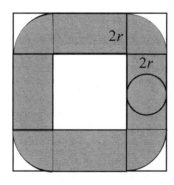

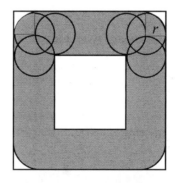

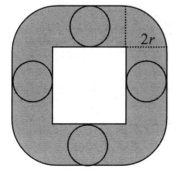

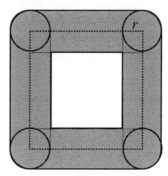

Figure out the difference in the areas between two figures.

PRACTICE

1. A disk of radius 1 rolls all the way around the inside of a square of side length $s > 4$ and sweeps out a region of area A. A second disk of radius 1 rolls all the way around the outside of the same square and sweeps out a region of area $2A$. The value of s can be written as $a + \dfrac{b\pi}{c}$, where a, b, and c are positive integers and b and c are relatively prime. What is $a + b + c$? (2021 AMC 10A #19)

(A) 10   (B) 11   (C) 12   (D) 13   (E) 14

| **16** | Polygon |

Polygon

In elementary geometry, a **polygon** is a plane figure that is described by a finite number of straight line segments connected to form a closed polygonal chain or polygonal circuit. The solid plane region, the bounding circuit, or the two together, may be called a **polygon**.

The segments of a polygonal circuit are called its *edges or sides,* and the points where two edges meet are the polygon's vertices (singular: vertex) or corners. The interior of a solid polygon is sometimes called its body. An ***n*-gon** is a polygon with n sides; for example, a triangle is a 3-gon.

Angles

Any polygon has as many corners as it has sides. Each corner has several angles. The two most important ones are:

Interior angle – The sum of the interior angles of a simple *n*-gon is

$$(n-2)\pi \text{ radians } \text{ or } (n-2) \times 180 \text{ degrees.}$$

Exterior angle – The exterior angle is the supplementary angle to the interior angle. the sum of the exterior angles is 360°.

PRACTICE

1. Points $A, B, C,$ and D lie on a line, in that order, with $AB = CD$ and $BC = 12$. Point E is not on the line, and $BE = CE = 10$. The perimeter of $\triangle AED$ is twice the perimeter of $\triangle BEC$. Find AB. (2002 AMC 10A #23)

   (A) $\frac{15}{2}$ (B) 8   (C) $\frac{17}{2}$ (D) 9   (E) $\frac{19}{2}$

2. In trapezoid $ABCD$ with bases $\overline{AB}$ and $\overline{CD}$, we have $AB = 52$, $BC = 12$, $CD = 39$ and $DA = 5$ (diagram not to scale). The area of $ABCD$ is   (2002 AMC 10A #25)

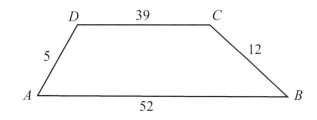

   (A) 182   (B) 195   (C) 210   (D) 234   (E) 260

3. A regular octagon $ABCDEFGH$ has sides of length two. Find the area of $\triangle ADG$. (2002 AMC 10B #17)

   (A) $4+2\sqrt{2}$ (B) $6+\sqrt{2}$ (C) $4+3\sqrt{2}$ (D) $3+4\sqrt{2}$ (E) $8+\sqrt{2}$

4. In square $ABCD$, points E and H lie on $\overline{AB}$ and $\overline{DA}$, respectively, so that $AE = AH$. Points F and G lie on $\overline{BC}$ and $\overline{CD}$, respectively, and points I and J lie on $\overline{EH}$ so that $\overline{FI} \perp \overline{EH}$ and $\overline{GJ} \perp \overline{EH}$. See the figure below. Triangle AEH, quadrilateral $BFIE$, quadrilateral $DHJG$, and pentagon $FCGJI$ each has area 1. What is FI^2?
   (2010 AMC 10B #21)

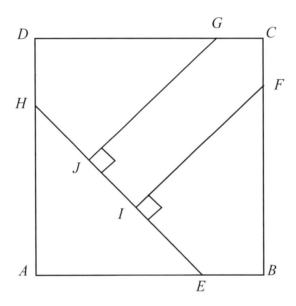

   (A) $\dfrac{7}{3}$ (B) $8-4\sqrt{2}$ (C) $1+\sqrt{2}$ (D) $\dfrac{7\sqrt{2}}{4}$ (E) $2\sqrt{2}$

5. As shown in the figure below, point E lies on the opposite half-plane determined by line CD from point A so that $\angle CDE = 110°$. Point F lies on $\overline{AD}$ so that $DE = DF$, and $ABCD$ is a square. What is the degree measure of $\angle AFE$? (2001 AMC 10A #7)

   (A) 160   (B) 164   (C) 166   (D) 170   (E) 174

| **17** | Graphs of $|x|+|y|=c$ and $|x|-|y|=c$ |

Example 1: Graph of $|x|+|y|=1$

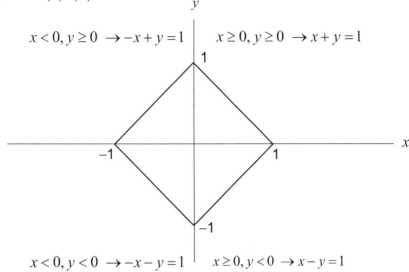

$x<0, y\geq 0 \rightarrow -x+y=1$ $x\geq 0, y\geq 0 \rightarrow x+y=1$

$x<0, y<0 \rightarrow -x-y=1$ $x\geq 0, y<0 \rightarrow x-y=1$

Example 2: Graph of $|x|-|y|=1$ Example 3: Graph of $|x|-|y|=-1$

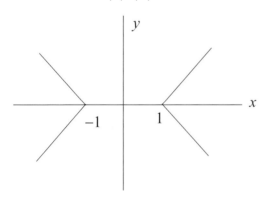   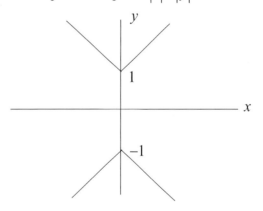

PRACTICE

1. How many ordered pairs of real numbers (x, y) satisfy the following system of equations?

$$x+3y=3$$

$$\big||x|-|y|\big|=1$$

(A) 1   (B) 2   (C) 3   (D) 4   (E) 8

2. If $|x|+|y|=4$ and $P=2x+y$, what is the maximum value of P?

(A) 1   (B) 2   (C) 3   (D) 4   (E) 8

3. How many ordered pairs (x, y) of real numbers satisfy the following system of equations?

$$x^2 + 3y = 9$$

$$\left(|x| + |y| - 4\right)^2 = 1$$

(A) 1   (B) 2   (C) 3   (D) 5   (E) 7

18	Identical Equation

An **identity equation** is an equation that is always true for any value substituted into the variable.

1. Both sides of the equation have same expression.

Example:

If $8(x+2)+3x=(a+b)x+b$ is true for all values of x, what is the value of a and b?

Solution) $8(x+2)+3x=(a+b)x+b$ → $11x+16=(a+b)x+b$

Identical equation coefficients of variable is equal.

$11=a+b$ and $b=16$, therefore $a=-5$.

PRACTICE

1. Find the value(s) of x such that $8xy-12y+2x-3=0$ is true for all values of y.
   (AMC 2002 10B #13)

(A) $\dfrac{2}{3}$ (B) $\dfrac{3}{2}$ or $-\dfrac{1}{4}$ (C) $-\dfrac{2}{3}$ or $-\dfrac{1}{4}$ (D) $\dfrac{3}{2}$ (E) $-\dfrac{3}{2}$ or $-\dfrac{1}{4}$

2. If $xy-10x+24y=2x+288$ is true for all values of y, what is the value of x?

(A) 12   (B) −12   (C) 24   (D) −24   (E) 36

19 | Average Speed (Average Rate of Change)

The **average speed** of an object is the total distance traveled by the object divided by the elapsed time to cover that distance. It's a scalar quantity which means it is defined only by magnitude.

Average speed uses the formula:

$$\text{Average Speed} = \frac{\text{Total Distance}}{\text{Total Time}}$$

Example:

John drove for 3 hours at a rate of 50 miles per hour and for 4 hours at 60 miles per hour. What was his average speed for the whole journey?

Total Distance $= 50 \times 3 + 60 \times 4 = 390$,   Total Time $= 3 + 4 = 7$

Average Speed $= \dfrac{390}{7}$ mph

PRACTICE

1. Mr. Earl E. Bird leaves home every day at 8:00 AM to go to work. If he drives at an average speed of 40 miles per hour, he will be late by 3 minutes. If he drives at an average speed of 60 miles per hour, he will be early by 3 minutes. How many miles per hour does Mr. Bird need to drive to get to work exactly on time? (2002 AMC 10A #12)

   (A) 45   (B) 48   (C) 50   (D) 55   (E) 58

20 | Relative Speed

Relative Speed "Relative" means **"in comparison to"**. Thus, the concept of relative speed is used when two or more bodies moving with some speeds are considered.

Relative" means "in comparison to". Thus, the concept of relative speed is used when two or more bodies moving with some speeds are considered. To make things simpler, one body can be made stationary and take the speed of the other body with respect to the stationary body, which is the sum of the speeds if the bodies are moving in the opposite direction and the difference if they are moving in the same direction. This speed of the moving body with respect to the stationary body is called the relative Speed.

Speed of object 1 = v_1 Speed of object 2 = v_2 $v_1 > v_2$

1. When the Objects are moving in the same Direction

   Relative speed of object 1 $= v_1 - v_2$

2. When the Objects are moving in the same Direction

   Relative speed of object 1 $= v_1 + v_2$

PRACTICE

1. Emily sees a ship traveling at a constant speed along a straight section of a river. She walks parallel to the riverbank at a uniform rate faster than the ship. She counts 210 equal steps walking from the back of the ship to the front. Walking in the opposite direction, she counts 42 steps of the same size from the front of the ship to the back. In terms of Emily's equal steps, what is the length of the ship? (2021 AMC 10A #11)

   (A) 70   (B) 84   (C) 98   (D) 105   (E) 126

21	Algebra with Integer solutions (Special equations)

When we have **a single equation** that has **several variables** can be solved by the constraint such as the variables are integers.

Generally, we have three different types.

1. $x^2 - y^2 = (x+y)(x-y)$

   Example: If $a^2 - b^2 = 3$, where, a, b are positive integers, find the values of a and b.

   Solution) $(a+b)(a-b) = 3 \rightarrow a+b = 3$ and $a-b = 1$
   Therefore, $a = 2, b = 1$.

2. $xy + ax + by = (x+b)(y+a) - ab$

   Example: If $xy - x + y = 6$, where x, y are positive integers, find the values of x and y.

   Solution) $xy - x + y = 6 \rightarrow x(y-1) + (y-1) = 5 \rightarrow (x+1)(y-1) = 5$

   $\begin{cases} x+1 = 5 \\ y-1 = 1 \end{cases} \rightarrow x = 4, y = 2$ or $\begin{cases} x+1 = 1 \\ y-1 = 5 \end{cases} \rightarrow x = 0, y = 6$ (not integer)

   Therefore, $x = 4$ and $y = 2$.

3. $(\quad)^2 + (\quad)^2 = k$.

   Example: If $x^2 + y^2 - 2y = 0$, where x and y are positive integers, find the values of x and y.

   Solution) $x^2 + y^2 - 2y + 1 = 1 \rightarrow x^2 + (y-1)^2 = 1$,

   $\begin{cases} x^2 = 1 \\ (y-1)^2 = 0 \end{cases} \rightarrow x = 1, y = 1$

PRACTICE

1. $a^2 - b^2 = 9$, where a and b are positive integers, and $a > b$. Find the values of a and b.

2. Find the values of positive integers of a and b such that $\dfrac{1}{a} + \dfrac{1}{b} = \dfrac{1}{13}$, where $a > b$.

3. Given that x and y are distinct nonzero real numbers such that $x + \dfrac{2}{x} = y + \dfrac{2}{y}$, what is xy?

   (2013 AMC 12A #8)

   (A) $\dfrac{1}{4}$ (B) $\dfrac{1}{2}$ (C) 1   (D) 2   (E) 4

4. Real numbers x and y satisfy the equation $x^2 + y^2 = 10x - 6y - 34$. What is $x + y$?
   (2013 AMC 12B #6)

   (A) 1   (B) 2   (C) 3   (D) 6   (E) 8

5. There are exactly N distinct rational numbers k such that $|k| < 200$ and
   $$5x^2 + kx + 12 = 0$$
   has at least one integer solution for x. What is N? (2014 AMC 12A #19)

   (A) 6   (B) 12   (C) 24   (D) 48   (E) 78

6. For how many positive integers n is $\dfrac{n}{30-n}$ also a positive integer? (2014 AMC 12B #7)

   (A) 4   (B) 5   (C) 6   (D) 7   (E) 8

7. Integers x and y with $x > y > 0$ satisfy $x + y + xy = 80$. What is x? (2015 12A #10)

   (A) 8   (B) 10   (C) 15   (D) 18   (E) 26

8. For how many (not necessarily positive) integer values of n is the value of $4000 \cdot \left(\dfrac{2}{5}\right)^n$ an integer? (2018 AMC 10A #7, 2018 AMC 12A #7)

   (A) 3   (B) 4   (C) 6   (D) 8   (E) 9

9. Positive real numbers a and b have the property that $\sqrt{\log a} + \sqrt{\log b} + \log \sqrt{a} + \log \sqrt{b} = 100$ and all four terms on the left are positive integers, where $\log$ denotes the base 10 logarithm. What is ab?

(A) 10^{52} (B) 10^{100} (C) 10^{144} (D) 10^{164} (E) 10^{200}

10. How many ordered pairs of integers (x, y) satisfy the equation $x^{2020} + y^2 = 2y$?
    (2020 AMC 10B #9)

(A) 1 (B) 2 (C) 3 (D) 4 (E) infinitely many

11. Real numbers x and y satisfy the equation $x^2 + y^2 = 10x - 6y - 34$. . What is $x + y$?
    (2013 AMC 10B #11)

(A) 1 (B) 2 (C) 3 (D) 6 (E) 8

12. How many ordered pairs (a, b) of positive integers satisfy the equation
$$a \cdot b + 63 = 20 \cdot \text{lcm}(a,b) + 12 \cdot \gcd(a,b),$$
where $\gcd(a,b)$ denotes the greatest common divisor of a and b, and $\text{lcm}(a,b)$ denotes their least common multiple? (2018 10B #23)

(A) 0 (B) 2 (C) 4 (D) 6 (E) 8

13. The zeroes of the function $f(x) = x^2 - ax + 2a$ are integers. What is the sum of the possible values of a? (2015 AMC 10 A #23)

(A) 7 (B) 8 (C) 16 (D) 17 (E) 18

14. A two-digit positive integer is said to be *cuddly* if it is equal to the sum of its nonzero tens digit and the square of its units digit. How many two-digit positive integers are cuddly?

(A) 0 (B) 1 (C) 2 (D) 3 (E) 4

| **22** | Absolute Value Equation |

Rule 1) Solve the equation: $|3x - 5| = 10$

$$3x - 5 = 10, -10 \rightarrow 3x = 15, -5 \rightarrow x = 5, -\frac{5}{3}$$

Rule 2) Solve the equation: $|3x - 5| = -10$

Absolute value cannot be negative. $\rightarrow$ No Solution

Rule 3) Some absolute value equations have variables both sides of the equation.
Solve the equation: $|3x - 6| = x + 4$

Use piece-wise function as follows.

$$|3x - 6| = \begin{cases} x \geq 2, & 3x - 6 = x + 4 \rightarrow 2x = 10 \rightarrow x = 5 \, (OK) : 5 \text{ is greater than 2.} \\ \\ x < 2, & -3x + 6 = x + 4 \rightarrow 2 = 4x \rightarrow x = \frac{1}{2} \, (OK) : \frac{1}{2} \text{ is less than 2.} \end{cases}$$

The answer is $x = 5$, $x = \frac{1}{2}$.

PRACTICE

1. Solve the equation $|x - 6| = 2x + 8$.

2. Solve the equation $\left| 2x - |10 - 2x| \right| = x$.

3. What is the sum of all the solutions of $x = \left| 2x - |60 - 2x| \right|$? (2010 AMC 10B #13)

    (A) 32   (B) 60   (C) 92   (D) 120   (E) 124

4. What is the product of all the roots of the equation $\sqrt{5|x| + 8} = \sqrt{x^2 - 16}$? (2011 AMC 10B #19)

    (A) –64   (B) –24   (C) –9   (D) 24   (E) 576

23	# Discriminant

Discriminants describe the nature of the roots of a quadratic function.

Given the quadratic function $f(x) = ax^2 + bx + c$, the roots of $ax^2 + bx + c = 0$ is

$$x = \frac{-b \pm \sqrt{b^2 - 4ac}}{2a}$$

Let $D = b^2 - 4ac$ → Discriminant: Tell us the nature of the roots.

The graph of each case is as follows.

1) $D > 0$,   2) $D = 0$ 3) $D < 0$

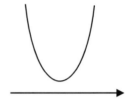

Two distinct real roots   One real root (equal)   No real roots (two imaginary roots)

PRACTICE

1. How many ordered pairs of positive integers (b, c) exist where both

   $x^2 + bx + c = 0$ and $x^2 + cx + b = 0$ do not have distinct, real solutions?
   (2021 AMC 10A #20)

   (A) 4   (B) 6   (C) 8   (D) 10   (E) 12

24	Simplifying Complex Radical

If we have a complex radical expression as follows, it can be simplified in a simple radical expression.

1. $\sqrt{(a+b)+2\sqrt{ab}} = \sqrt{a}+\sqrt{b}$

2. $\sqrt{(a+b)-2\sqrt{ab}} = \sqrt{a}-\sqrt{b}$ $(a>b)$

Example

1. $\sqrt{8+\sqrt{48}} = \sqrt{(6+2)+2\sqrt{12}} = \sqrt{6}+\sqrt{2}$

2. $\sqrt{11-4\sqrt{7}} = \sqrt{(7+4)-2\sqrt{28}} = \sqrt{7}-\sqrt{4} = \sqrt{7}-2$

PRACTICE

1. Which of the following is equal to $\sqrt{9-6\sqrt{2}} + \sqrt{9+6\sqrt{2}}$? (2011 AMC 10A #16)

   (A) $3\sqrt{2}$ (B) $2\sqrt{6}$ (C) $\dfrac{7\sqrt{2}}{2}$ (D) $3\sqrt{3}$ (E) 6

2. Evaluate $\sqrt{18-8\sqrt{2}} + \sqrt{38+12\sqrt{2}}$.

   (A) 4   (B) $4\sqrt{2}$ (C) 8   (D) $8\sqrt{2}$ (E) 10

3. $\left| \sqrt{12-8\sqrt{2}} - \sqrt{12+8\sqrt{2}} \right| =$

   (A) 4   (B) $4\sqrt{2}$ (C) 8   (D) $8\sqrt{2}$ (E) 12

25	Sum of Digits of a Number

Example: What is the sum of the digits of $2^{24} \cdot 25^{20}$?

Solution) $16^6 \cdot 25^{10} = 2^{24} \cdot 5^{20} = 2^{20} \cdot 5^{20} \cdot 2^4 = (2 \cdot 5)^{20} \cdot 16 = 16 \times 10^{20}$

Sum of the digits is $1 + 6 = 7$.

PRACTICE

1. The number $25^{64} \cdot 64^{25}$ is the square of a positive integer N. In decimal representation, the sum of the digits of N is   (2002 AMC 10B #16)

    (A) 7   (B) 14   (C) 21   (D) 28   (E) 35

2. In decimal representation, what is the sum of the digits of

$$2^{30} \times 4^8 \times 25^{25} ?$$

    (A) 8   (B) 10   (C) 11   (D) 13   (E) 15

| 26 | How to solve $ax + by = c$ |

Example 1

How many pairs (x, y) are there to express 1002 in the form of $2x + 3y = 1002$, where x and y are nonnegative integers?

Solution) $y = \dfrac{1002 - 2x}{3} = \dfrac{2(501 - x)}{3}$ $\rightarrow$ We can see $(501 - x)$ must be multiples of 3 so that we will get an integer y. We also can see the minimum of $(501 - x)$ is 0 when $x = 501$, and the maximum of $(501 - x)$ is 501 when $x = 0$. The number of the multiples of 3 on $[0, 501]$ is $\left\lfloor \dfrac{501}{3} \right\rfloor + 1 = 168$. Therefore, the number of y satisfying the constraints is 168. So, the number of pairs (x, y) is also 168.

PRACTICE

1. How many ways are there to write 2016 as the sum of twos and threes, ignoring order? (For example, $1008 \cdot 2 + 0 \cdot 3$ and $402 \cdot 2 + 404 \cdot 3$ are two such ways.) (2016 AMC 10A #14)

    (A) 236   (B) 336   (C) 337   (D) 403   (E) 672

2. How many ways are there to write 2016 as the sum of threes and fours, ignoring order?

    (A) 169   (B) 170   (C) 171   (D) 172   (E) 173

3. How many pairs of (a, b) are there to satisfy the equation, $2a + 5b = 2020$ where a and b are positive integers?

    (A) 200   (B) 201   (C) 202   (D) 404   (E) 1010

No Material

27 | Vieta's Formulas

In mathematics, **Vieta's formulas** are formulas that relate the coefficients of a polynomial to sums and products of its roots. Named after François Viète (more commonly referred to by the Latinized form of his name, **Franciscus Vieta**), the formulas are used specifically in algebra.

Any general polynomial of degree n

$$f(x) = a_n x^n + a_{n-1} x^{n-1} + a_{n-2} x^{n-2} + \cdots + a_1 x + a_0 = 0$$

(with the coefficients being real or complex numbers and $a_n \neq 0$) is known by the <u>fundamental theorem of algebra</u> to have n (not necessarily distinct) complex roots $r_1, r_2, r_3, \cdots, r_n$. Vieta's formulas relate the polynomial's coefficients $\{a_k\}$ to signed sums of products of its roots $\{r_i\}$

as follows:

Sum of the roots:

1) $r_1 + r_2 + r_3 + \cdots + r_n = -\dfrac{a_{n-1}}{a_n}$

2) $\left(r_1 r_2 + r_1 r_3 + r_1 r_3 + \cdots + r_1 r_n \right) + \left(r_2 r_3 + r_2 r_4 + r_2 r_5 + \cdots + r_2 r_n \right) + \cdots + r_{n-1} r_n = \dfrac{a_{n-2}}{a_n}$

Product of the roots:

$$r_1 r_2 r_3 \cdots r_n = (-1)^n \dfrac{a_0}{a_n}$$

Example: For the equation $x^4 + 3x^2 - 4 = 0$, r_1, r_2, r_3, r_4 are the roots of the equation.

Coefficients: $a_4 = 1$, $a_3 = 0$, $a_2 = 3$, $a_1 = 0$, $a_0 = -4$

Sum and Product of the roots:

1) $r_1 + r_2 + r_3 + r_4 = -\dfrac{a_3}{a_4} = -\dfrac{0}{1} = 0$

2) $r_1 r_2 + r_1 r_3 + r_1 r_4 + r_2 r_3 + r_2 r_4 + r_3 + r_4 = \dfrac{a_2}{a_4} = \dfrac{3}{1} = 3$

3) $r_1 r_2 r_3 + r_1 r_2 r_4 + r_1 r_3 r_4 + r_2 r_3 r_4 = -\dfrac{a_1}{a_4} = -\dfrac{0}{1} = 0$

4) $r_1 r_2 r_3 r_4 = \dfrac{a_0}{a_4} = \dfrac{(-4)}{1} = -4$

PRACTICE

1. If α and β are the roots of the equation $x^2 + 5x - 3 = 0$, find the value of $\alpha^2 + \beta^2$.

2. If r_1, r_2 are the roots of the equation $x^2 - 7x - 10 = 0$, what is the value of $\dfrac{1}{r_1} + \dfrac{1}{r_2}$?

3. If α, β are the roots of the equation $x^2 - 8x + 11 = 0$, what is the value of

$$\alpha^3 + \beta^3 + \alpha^2 + \beta^2 + \alpha + \beta \ ?$$

4. If $r_1, r_2,$ and r_3 are the roots of the equation $x^3 - 2x^2 + 5x - 7 = 0$, what is the value of

$$r_1^2 + r_2^2 + r_3^2 \ ?$$

5. What is the sum of all the roots of $(2x+3)(x-4) + (2x+3)(x-6) = 0$?
   (2002 AMC 10 #10, AMC 12 #1)

   (A) $\dfrac{7}{2}$ (B) 4   (C) 5   (D) 7   (E) 13

6. Both roots of the quadratic equation $x^2 - 63x + k = 0$ are prime numbers. The number of possible values of k is   (2002 AMC 10A #14)

   (A) 0   (B) 1   (C) 2   (D) 4   (E) more than 4

7. Let d and e denote the solutions of $2x^2 + 3x - 5 = 0$. What is the value of $(d-1)(e-1)$?
   (2003 AMC 10A #5)

   (A) $-\dfrac{5}{2}$ (B) 0   (C) 3   (D) 5   (E) 6

8. For a certain complex number c, the polynomial
   $$P(x) = \left(x^2 - 2x + 2\right)\left(x^2 - Cx + 4\right)\left(x^2 - 4x + 8\right)$$
   has exactly 4 distinct roots. What is $|C|$?   (2019 AMC 12A #14)

   (A) 2   (B) $\sqrt{6}$ (C) $2\sqrt{2}$ (D) 3   (E) $\sqrt{10}$

9. Let p, q, and r be the distinct roots of the polynomial $x^3 - 22x + 80x - 67$. It is given that there exist real numbers $A, B,$ and C such that $\dfrac{1}{s^3 - 22s^2 + 80s - 67} = \dfrac{A}{s-p} + \dfrac{B}{s-q} + \dfrac{C}{s-r}$ for all $s \notin \{p, q, r\}$. What is $\dfrac{1}{A} + \dfrac{1}{B} + \dfrac{1}{C}$? (2019 AMC 10A #24)

   (A) 243   (B) 244   (C) 245   (D) 256   (E) 247

10. The polynomial $x^3 - ax^2 + bx - 2010 = 0$ has three positive integer roots. What is the smallest possible value of a? (2010 AMC 10A #21)

   (A) 78   (B) 88   (C) 98   (D) 108   (E) 118

11. Let a and b be the roots of the equation $x^2 - mx + 2 = 0$. Suppose that $a + \left(\dfrac{1}{b}\right)$ and $b + \left(\dfrac{1}{a}\right)$ are the roots of the equation $x^2 - px + q = 0$. What is q?

   (A) $\dfrac{5}{2}$ (B) $\dfrac{7}{2}$ (C) 4   (D) $\dfrac{9}{2}$ (E) 8

12. What is the sum of the reciprocals of the roots of the equation
$$\frac{2003}{2004}x + 1 + \frac{1}{x} = 0 ?$$
(2003 AMC 10A #18)

   (A) $-\dfrac{2003}{2004}$ (B) -1 (C) $\dfrac{2003}{2004}$ (D) 1   (E) $\dfrac{2004}{2003}$

28	LCM and GCF(GCD)

1) Factorization

To find either the Least Common Multiple (LCM) or Greatest Common Factor (GCF or GCD: Divisor) of two numbers, you always start out the same way: you find the prime <u>factorizations</u> of the two numbers.

$$\begin{cases} 800 = 2^5 \cdot 5^2 \\ 1800 = 2^3 \cdot 3^2 \cdot 5^2 \end{cases} \rightarrow \text{GCF} = 2^3 \cdot 5^2 = 200, \ \text{LCM} = 2^5 \cdot 3^2 \cdot 5^2 = 7200$$

2) Ladder

$$\begin{array}{r|rr} 100 & 800 & 1800 \\ \hline 2 & 8 & 18 \\ \hline & 4 & 9 \end{array} \rightarrow \text{GCF} = 100 \cdot 2 = 200, \ \text{LCM} = 100 \cdot 2 \cdot 4 \cdot 9 = 7200$$

3) Common divisor

$$\text{GCF}(800,1800) = 100\text{GCF}(8,18) = 100(2) = 200$$

$$\text{LCM}(800,1800) = 100\text{LCM}(8,18) = 100 \cdot 72 = 7200$$

<u>Important property</u>

The product of two natural numbers is equal to the product of their GCD and LCM.

$$m \times n = \text{GCD}(m,n) \cdot \text{LCM}(m,n)$$

Example: Find the product of the GCD and the LCM of 100 and 120.

Solution) $\text{GCD} \times \text{LCM} = 100 \times 120 = 12000$
Check:
$$\text{GCD}(100,120) = 10\text{GCD}(10,12) = 10(2) = 20$$
$$\text{LCM}(100,120) = 10\text{LCM}(10,12) = 10(60) = 600$$
$$\text{GCD}(100,120) \cdot \text{LCM}(100,120) = 12000$$

Remember:

$$\begin{array}{r|cc} \text{GCD} & a & b \\ \hline & k_1 & k_2 \end{array}$$

1. $\text{LCM} = k_1 \cdot k_2 \cdot \text{GCD}$ 2. k_1 and k_2 are relatively prime 3. LCM is a multiple of GCD.

PRACTICE

1. Find m if $\gcd(m, 40) = 10$ and $\operatorname{lcm}(m, 40) = 280$.

2. The LCM of a pair of natural numbers is 450, and the GCD of the numbers is 6. If one of the number is 18, what is the other number?

3. If $\operatorname{LCM}(a, b)$ is 1600 and $\operatorname{GCD}(a, b)$ is 40, then how many ordered pairs (a, b) of positive integers are possible?

   (A) 0   (B) 1   (C) 2   (D) 3   (E) 4

4. How many ordered pairs (a, b) of positive integers satisfy the equation
$$a \cdot b + 63 = 20 \cdot \operatorname{lcm}(a, b) + 12 \cdot \gcd(a, b),$$
   where $\gcd(a, b)$ denotes the greatest common divisor of a and b, and $\operatorname{lcm}(a, b)$ denotes their least common multiple? (2018 10B #23)

   (A) 0   (B) 2   (C) 4   (D) 6   (E) 8

5. Let n be the least positive integer greater than 1000 for which
$$\gcd(63, n + 120) = 21 \quad \text{and} \quad \gcd(n + 63, 120) = 60.$$
   What is the sum of the digits? (2020 AMC 10A #24)

   (A) 12   (B) 15   (C) 18   (D) 21   (E) 24

29	Modular Arithmetic

Definition:

The integers a and b are congruent modulo m if and only if $a - b$ is divisible by m. This congruence is written as:

$$a \equiv b \bmod m$$

where, m is a positive integer greater than 1 and is called modulus.

When a and b are divided by m, the same remainder is obtained. The sign "$\equiv$" indicates congruence.

Example

1) In the 12-hour clock system, 15 and 3 are congruence modulo 12.

$16 \equiv 4 \bmod 12$ (You can add or subtract 12 in any side of the equation.)
$28 \equiv 4 \bmod 12$, $\quad 16 \equiv 16 \bmod 12$, $\quad 28 \equiv 16 \bmod 12$

2) In the 7-day week system, a modulo 7 system applies.

Q) If today is **Friday**, what day will it be 120 days from today?

Answer: $120 \equiv 1 \bmod 7$. That is 120 days from today is **Saturday**.

Theorem

Theorem 1: If $a \equiv r \bmod b$ and $0 \le r < b$, then $a = qb + r$, where q is the quotient.

Theorem 2: If $a \equiv b \bmod m$ and $c \equiv d \bmod m$, then

a) $a \pm c \equiv b \pm d \bmod m$ b) $a \times c \equiv b \times d \bmod m$.

Example: $15 \equiv 1 \bmod 7$ and $10 \equiv 3 \bmod 7$, then

1) $15 + 10 \equiv (1 + 3) \bmod 7 \;\rightarrow\; 25 \equiv 4 \bmod 7$

2) $15 - 10 \equiv (1 - 3) \bmod 7 \;\rightarrow\; 5 \equiv -2 \bmod 7 \equiv 5 \bmod 7$

3) $15 \times 10 \equiv (1 \times 3) \bmod 7 \;\rightarrow\; 150 \equiv 3 \bmod 7$

Theorem 3: If $a \equiv b \bmod lcm(m_1, m_2, m_3, \cdots m_k)$, then $a \equiv b \bmod (m_i) \; i = 1, 2, 3, \cdots k$.

Example: 30 is $lcm(3, 5, 6)$.

If $35 \equiv 5 \bmod 30$,

then $35 \equiv 5 \bmod 3$ or, $35 \equiv 5 \bmod 5$ or $35 \equiv 5 \bmod 6$.

Theorem 4: If $a \equiv b \bmod m$ and $a \equiv b \bmod n$, then $a \equiv b \bmod lcm(m,n.)$

Example: $31 \equiv 3 \bmod 4$ and $31 \equiv 3 \bmod 7$, then $31 \equiv 3 \bmod 28$.

Theorem 5: If $a \equiv b \bmod m$, then $a^k \equiv b^k \bmod m$.

Example: If $31 = 1 \bmod 10$, then $31^{100} = 1^{100} \bmod 10$.

Theorem 6: If $ac \equiv bc \bmod m$ and $\gcd(c,m) = 1$, then $a \equiv b \bmod m$.

Example: If $30 \equiv 9 \bmod 7$, then $10 \equiv 3 \bmod 7$.

Theorem 7: If $N = r \bmod 6$, then $N^3 = r \bmod 6$.

Example: If $1+3+4 = 2 \bmod 6$, then $1^3 + 3^3 + 4^3 = 2 \bmod 6$.

Theorem 8: $10^k a \equiv a \bmod 9$

If $N = abcd$, then $N \equiv (a+b+c+d) \bmod 9$.

Example: $3672 \equiv (3+6+7+2) \bmod 9 \;\rightarrow\; 18 \bmod 9 \;\rightarrow\; 0 \bmod 9$

Remember: $3000 \equiv 3 \bmod 9$, $600 \equiv 6 \bmod 9$, $70 \equiv 7 \bmod 9$, $2 \equiv 2 \bmod 9$

PRACTICE

1. If a number N divides each of 47 and 25 with the same remainder in each case, what is the largest value of N?

2. If a number N divides 37 with remainder of r and divides 54 with remainder $2r$, what is the largest value of N?

3. If a certain number is divided by 3,4,6, or 7, the remainder 2 in each case, what is the least number that satisfies the conditions?

4. If a certain number is divided by 2,3,4, or 5, the respective remainder are 1,2,3, and 4. What is the least number that satisfies these conditions?

5. The notation $a \equiv b \pmod n$ means $(a - b)$ is a multiple of n where n is a positive integer greater than one. Find the sum of all possible values of n such that both of the following are true: $171 \equiv 80 \pmod n$ and $468 \equiv 13 \pmod n$.

6. When n is divided by 2016, the remainder is 42. What is the remainder when n is divided by 24?

7. When a positive integer m is divided by 7, the remainder is 2; when a positive integer n is divided by 7, the remainder is 6. What is the remainder when $m \times n$ is divided by 7?

8. When two different numbers are divided by 7, remainders of 2 and 3, respectively, are left. What is the greatest possible three-digit product of these two numbers?

9. An integer has a remainder of 2 when divided by 6 and a remainder of 3 when divided by 7. Find the sum of all such integers from 1 to 1000.

10. a and b are positive integers. When a is divided by 7, the remainder is 2. When b is divided by 7, the remainder is 1. What is the remainder when $a^2 + b$ is divided by 7?

11. When the three integers 618, 343, and 277 are divided by a positive integer, d, where $d > 1$, the remainders are the same. What is the smallest possible value of d?

12. For a certain natural number n, n^2 gives a remainder of 4 when divided by 5, and n^3 gives a remainder of 2 when divided by 5. What remainder does n give when divided by 5?

13. When Rachel divides her favorite number by 7, she gets a remainder of 5. What will the remainder be if she multiplies her favorite number by 5 and then divides by 7?

14. What is the greatest three-digit number that is one more than a multiple of 7 and three more than a multiple of 5?

15. When a positive integer is divided by 7, the remainder is 4. When the same integer is divided by 9, the remainder is 3. What is the smallest possible value of this integer?

16. In year N, the 300th day of the year is a Tuesday. In year $N + 1$, the 200th day is also a Tuesday. On what day of the week did the 100th day of year $N - 1$ occur?
   (2000 AMC 10 #25, 2000 AMC 12 #18))

   (A) Thursday   (B) Friday   (C) Saturday   (D) Sunday   (E) Monday

17. A number m is randomly selected from the set $\{11, 13, 15, 17, 19\}$, and a number n is randomly selected from $\{1999, 2000, 2001, \cdots 2018\}$. What is the probability that m^n has a units digit of 1? (2018 AMC 10A #19)

(A) $\dfrac{1}{5}$ (B) $\dfrac{1}{4}$ (C) $\dfrac{3}{10}$ (D) $\dfrac{7}{20}$ (E) $\dfrac{2}{5}$

18. How many of the first 2018 numbers in the sequence 101, 1001, 10001, 100001, $\cdots$ are divisible by 101? (2018 AMC 10B #13)

(A) 253   (B) 504   (C) 505   (D) 506   (E) 1009

19. Let $a_1, a_2, \cdots, a_{2018}$ be a strictly increasing sequence of positive integers such that

$$a_1 + a_2 + \cdots + a_{2018} = 2018^{2018}.$$

What is the remainder when $a_1^3 + a_2^3 + \cdots + a_{2018}^3$ is divided by 6? (2018 AMC 10B #16)

(A) 0   (B) 1   (C) 2   (D) 3   (E) 4

20. Let $S(n)$ equal the sum of the digits of positive integer n. For example, $S(1507) = 13$. For a particular positive integer n, $S(n) = 1274$. Which of the following could be the value of $S(n+1)$? (2017 AMC 10A #20)

(A) 1   (B) 3   (C) 12   (D) 1239   (E) 1265

21. What is the units digit of 13^{2003}? (2003 AMC 10A #16)

(A) 1   (B) 3   (C) 7   (D) 8   (E) 9

22. What is the tens digit in the sum $(7! + 8! + 9! + \cdots + 2006!)$? (2006 AMC 10B #11)

(A) 1   (B) 3   (C) 4   (D) 6   (E) 9

23. What is the remainder when $3^0 + 3^1 + 3^2 + \cdots 3^{2009}$ is divided by 8? (2009 AMC 10B #21)

(A) 0   (B) 1   (C) 2   (D) 4   (E) 6

24. Marvin had a birthday on Tuesday, May 27 in the leap year 2008. In what year will his birthday next fall on a Saturday? (2010 AMC 10A #10)

(A) 2011   (B) 2012   (C) 2013   (D) 2015   (E) 2017

25. Positive integers a, b, and c are randomly and independently selected with replacement from the set $\{1, 2, 3, \cdots, 2010\}$. What is the probability that $abc + ab + a$ is divisible by 3?
(2010 AMC 10B #18)

(A) $\dfrac{1}{3}$ (B) $\dfrac{29}{81}$ (C) $\dfrac{31}{81}$ (D) $\dfrac{11}{27}$ (E) $\dfrac{13}{27}$

26. Mrs. Walter gave an exam in mathematics class of five students. She entered the scores in random order into a spreadsheet, which recalculated the class average after each score entered. Mrs. Walter noticed that after each score entered, the average was always an integer. The scores (listed in ascending order) were 71, 76, 80, 82, and 91. What was the last score Mrs. Walter entered. (2000 AMC 10 #14)

(A) 71   (B) 76   (C) 80   (D) 82   (E) 91

27. How many distinct four-digit numbers are divisible by 3 and have 23 as their last two digits? (2003 AMC 10B #25)

(A) 27   (B) 30   (C) 33   (D) 81   (E) 91

28. Let n be the least positive integer greater than 1000 for which $\gcd(63, n + 120) = 21$ and $\gcd(n + 63, 120) = 60$. What is the sum of the digits of n? (2020 AMC 10 A #24)

(A) 12   (B) 15   (C) 18   (D) 21   (E) 24

29. The base-nine representation of the number N is $27{,}006{,}000{,}052_{\text{nine}}$. What is the remainder when N is divided by 5? (2021 AMC 10A #12)

(A) 0   (B) 0   (C) 2   (D) 3   (E) 4

30	**Sequence and Series**

1) Arithmetic Sequence with common difference d

$$a_n = a_1 + (n-1)d \ \rightarrow \ n = \frac{a_n - a_1}{d} + 1$$

$$S_n = \frac{(a_1 + a_n)n}{2}$$

Example
Find the number of even integers between 45 and 317?

Solution)

$a_1 = 46$, $a_n = 316$, and $d = 2$ $\ \rightarrow \ n = \dfrac{316 - 46}{2} = 135$ even integers

2) Geometric Sequence with common ratio r

$$a_n = a_1 r^{n-1}$$

$$S_n = \frac{a_1 (1 - r^n)}{1 - r}$$

3) Infinite Geometric Series

If $|r| < 1$, then $S_\infty = \dfrac{a_1}{1 - r}$.

1. A large equilateral triangle is constructed by using toothpicks to create rows of small equilateral triangles. For example, in the figure we have 3 rows of small congruent equilateral triangles, with 5 small triangles in the base row. How many toothpicks would be needed to construct a large equilateral triangle if the base row of the triangle consists of 2003 small equilateral triangles? (2003 AMC10A #23)

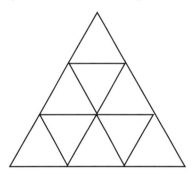

(A) 1,004,004   (B) 1,005,006   (C) 1,507,509   (D) 3,015,018   (E) 6,021,018

2. A sequence of three real numbers forms an arithmetic progression with a first term of 9. If 2 is added to the second term and 20 is added to the third term, the three resulting numbers form a geometric progression. What is the smallest possible value for the third term in the geometric progression? (2004 AMC 10A #18)

(A) 1   (B) 4   (C) 36   (D) 49   (E) 81

3. Let $a_1, a_2,...,$ be a sequence with the following properties.

(i) $a_1 = 1$, and

(ii) $a_{2^n} = n \cdot a_n$ for any positive integer n.

What is the value of $a_{2^{100}}$?

(A) 1   (B) 2^{99} (C) 2^{100} (D) 2^{4950} (E) 2^{9999}

31	Counting Techniques

A) Casework Counting

Casework is the process of splitting up a problem into a finite number of cases and then determining mathematical results for each respective case.

Example

How many pairs of positive integers (x, y) satisfy $x^2 + y < 30$?

Solution)

Case 1) If $x = 1$, then $1 + y < 30 \rightarrow y < 29 \rightarrow y = 1, 2, 3, \cdots 28 \rightarrow 28$ pairs

Case 2) If $x = 2$, then $4 + y < 30 \rightarrow y < 26 \rightarrow y = 1, 2, 3, \cdots 25 \rightarrow 25$ pairs

Case 3) If $x = 3$, then $9 + y < 30 \rightarrow y < 21 \rightarrow y = 1, 2, 3, \cdots 20 \rightarrow 20$ pairs

Case 4) If $x = 4$, then $16 + y < 30 \rightarrow y < 14 \rightarrow y = 1, 2, 3, \cdots 13 \rightarrow 13$ pairs

Case 5) If $x = 5$, then $25 + y < 30 \rightarrow y < 5 \rightarrow y = 1, 2, 3, 4 \rightarrow 4$ pairs

Therefore, total number of pairs is $28 + 25 + 20 + 13 + 4 = 90$ pairs.

B) Complementary Counting

Complementary counting is counting the complement of the set we want to count and subtracting that from the total number of possibilities. Complementary counting may lead to a quick solution.

PRACTICE

1. How many three-digit numbers are not multiple of 5? (Complementary counting)

2. How many three-digit numbers are not multiple of 3 or 4? (Complementary counting)

3. The Peter family has 3 sons and 2 daughters. In how many ways can they be seated in five chairs such that at least 2 boys are next to each other? (Complementary counting)

4. How many three-digit numbers have at least one zero? (Complementary counting)

5. Three young brother-sister pairs from different families need to take a trip in a van. These six children will occupy the second and third rows in the van, each of which has three seats. To avoid disruptions, siblings may not sit right next to each other in the same row, and no child may sit directly in front of his or her sibling. How many seating arrangements are possible for this trip? (2018 AMC 10B #18) (Casework)

(A) 60   (B) 72   (C) 92   (D) 96   (E) 120

6. A farmer's rectangular field is partitioned into 2 by 2 grid of 4 rectangular sections as shown in the figure. In each section the farmer will plant one crop: corn, wheat, soybeans, or potatoes. The farmer does not want to grow corn and wheat in any two sections that share a border, and the farmer does not want to grow soybeans and potatoes in any two sections that share a border. Given these restrictions, in how many ways can the farmer choose crops to plant in each of the four sections of the field?
(2021 AMC 10A #18)

(A) 12   (B) 64   (C) 84   (D) 90   (E) 144

1. How many ways are there to divide group of 12 people into 2 groups of 3 people and 3 groups of 2 people?

Solution)

$$\binom{12}{3}\binom{9}{3}\binom{6}{2}\binom{4}{2}\binom{2}{2}\frac{1}{2!}\cdot\frac{1}{3!} = \frac{12!}{3!(9!)}\cdot\frac{(9!)}{3!(6!)}\cdot\frac{(6!)}{2!(4!)}\cdot\frac{(4!)}{2!(2!)}\cdot\frac{(2!)}{2!(0!)}\cdot\frac{1}{2!}\cdot\frac{1}{3!}$$

$$= \frac{12!}{(3!)^2(2!)^3}\cdot\frac{1}{2!}\cdot\frac{1}{3!}$$

2. How many ways are there to divide group of 25 people into 5 groups of 5 people?

Solution)

$$\binom{25}{5}\binom{20}{5}\binom{15}{5}\binom{10}{5}\binom{5}{5}\frac{1}{5!} = \frac{25!}{5!(20!)}\cdot\frac{(20!)}{5!(15!)}\cdot\frac{(15!)}{5!(10!)}\cdot\frac{(10!)}{5!(5!)}\cdot\frac{(5!)}{5!0!}\cdot\frac{1}{5!}$$

$$= \frac{25!}{(5!)^6} = \frac{(5^2)!}{(5!)^6}$$

Let replace 5 with n. We got remarkably interesting formula as follows.

How many ways are there to divide group of n^2 people into n groups of n people?

$$\frac{(n^2)!}{(n!)^{n+1}} = \text{integer}$$

Example: How many ways are there to divide group of 49 people into 7 groups of 7 people?

Solution) The answer is $\dfrac{49!}{(7!)^8}$.

PRACTICE

1. In how many ways can 12 students be divided into 2 groups of 6 for a group project?

2. In how many ways can you divide 28 persons into three groups having 4, 12 and 12 persons?

3. How many ways can a class of 36 be divided into 6 equal groups?

4. How many ways can we divide 12 members into 3 equal groups?

5. How many ways can we divide 49 members into 7 equal groups?

6. How many ways can we divide 64 members into 8 equal groups?

7. For how many integers n between 1 and 50, inclusive, is $\dfrac{\left(n^2 - 1\right)!}{\left(n!\right)^n}$ an integer?

   (Recall that $0! = 1$.) (2019 AMC 10 #25)

   (A) 31   (B) 32   (C) 33   (D) 34   (E) 35

33	Counting multiples of a number

When we have a given interval $[1, n]$, the number of multiples of k is $\left\lfloor \dfrac{n}{k} \right\rfloor$.

Example 1

How many positive integers not exceeding 2019 are multiples of 11?

Solution) For the given interval $[1, 2019]$, the number of multiples of 11 is $\left\lfloor \dfrac{2019}{11} \right\rfloor = 183$.

Example 2

Let n is 5-digit number. How many numbers of n are divisible by 11?

Solution) For the given interval $[10000, 99999]$, the number of multiples of 11 is

$$\left\lfloor \frac{99999}{11} \right\rfloor - \left\lfloor \frac{9999}{11} \right\rfloor = 9090 - 909 = 8181.$$

PRACTICE

1. How many multiples of 7 are there between 300 and 900, inclusive.

2. How many positive integers not exceeding 2001 are multiples of 3 or 4 but not 5? (2001 AMC 10 #25)

   (A) 768   (B) 801   (C) 934   (D) 1067   (E) 1167

3. For how many integers n is $\dfrac{n}{20-n}$ the square of an integer? (2012 AMC 12B #12)

   (A) 1   (B) 2   (C) 3   (D) 4   (E) 10

4. Given that $3^8 \cdot 5^2 = a^b$ where both a and b are positive integers, find the smallest possible value for $a+b$. (2003 10B #14)

   (A) 25   (B) 34   (C) 351   (D) 407   (E) 900

5. Let S be the set of the 2005 smallest positive multiples of 4, and let T be the set of the 2005 smallest positive multiples of 6. How many elements are common to s and T? (2005 AMC 10A # 22)

   (A) 166   (B) 333   (C) 500   (D) 668   (E) 1001

6. How many numbers between 1 and 2005 are integer multiples of 3 or 4 but not 12?

   (2005 AMC 10B #13)

   (A) 501   (B) 668   (C) 835   (D) 1002   (E) 1169

7. Let n be a 5-digit number, and let q and r be the quotient and the remainder, respectively, when n is divided by 100. For how many values of n is $q+r$ divisible by 11?

   (2003 AMC 10A #25)

   (A) 8180   (B) 8181   (C) 8182   (D) 9000   (E) 9090

Multiple of 2^6 :				$\cdots 64 \cdots$		
Multiple of 2^5 :		$\cdots 32 \cdots$		$\cdots 64 \cdots$		
Multiple of 2^4 :	$\cdots 16 \cdots$	$\cdots 32 \cdots$	$\cdots 48 \cdots$	$\cdots 64 \cdots$	$\cdots 80 \cdots$	$\cdots 96 \cdots$
Multiple of 2^3 :	$\cdots 8 \cdots$ 16 24	$\cdots 32 \cdots$ 40 48 56		$\cdots 64 \cdots$ 72	80	88 96
Multiple of 2^2 :	4 8 12 16	$\cdots 32 \cdots$		$\cdots 64 \cdots$		
Multiple of 2 : 2 4 8$\cdots$		$\cdots 32 \cdots$		$\cdots 64 \cdots$		96 98 100

We can see that

$100! = 1 \cdot 2 \cdot 3 \cdot 4 \cdot 5 \cdot 6 \cdot 8 \cdot 9 \cdot 10 \cdots \cdot 96 \cdot 96 \cdot 97 \cdot 98 \cdot 99 \cdot 100$

$\qquad = 2(1 \cdot 2 \cdot 3 \cdot 4 \cdot 5 \cdots \cdot 46 \cdot 47 \cdot 48 \cdot 49 \cdot 50) = 2(50!) \rightarrow 50$ numbers are multiples of 2

$50! = 2(1 \cdot 2 \cdot 3 \cdot 4 \cdot 5 \cdots \cdot 23 \cdot 24 \cdot 25) = 2(25!) \rightarrow 25$ numbers are multiples of 2

$25! = 2(1 \cdot 2 \cdot 3 \cdot 4 \cdots \cdot 10 \cdot 11 \cdot 12) = 2(12!) \rightarrow 12$ numbers are multiples of 2

$12! = 2(1 \cdot 2 \cdot 3 \cdot 4 \cdot 5 \cdot 6) = 2(6!) \rightarrow 6$ numbers are multiples of 2

$6! = 2(1 \cdot 2 \cdot 3) = 2(3!) \rightarrow 3$ numbers are multiples of 2

$3! = 2(1) \rightarrow$ only one number is multiple of 2

Therefore, the exponent of the prime 2 is 50+25+12+6+3+1 = 97.

Formula to find the largest n such that 2^n divides 100! will be as follows.

Step 1) Find the number of multiple of 2 : $\left\lfloor \dfrac{100}{2} \right\rfloor = 50$

Step 2) Find the number of multiple of 2^2 : $\left\lfloor \dfrac{100}{4} \right\rfloor = 25$

Step 3) Find the number of multiple of 2^3 : $\left\lfloor \dfrac{100}{8} \right\rfloor = 12$

Step 4) Find the number of multiple of 2^4 : $\left\lfloor \dfrac{100}{16} \right\rfloor = 6$

Step 5) Find the number of multiple of 2^5 : $\left\lfloor \dfrac{100}{32} \right\rfloor = 3$

Step 6) Find the number of multiple of 2^6 : $\left\lfloor \dfrac{100}{64} \right\rfloor = 1$

Therefore, $n = 50+25+12+6+3+1 = 97$. $(100! = 2^{97} \cdot 3^a \cdot 5^b \cdots)$

Generally,

Let p is a prime. For any positive integer n, the exponent $E(n)$ of the prime p in the prime factorization of $n!$ is

$$E_p(n) = \sum_{k=1}^{\infty} \left\lfloor \frac{n}{p} \right\rfloor = \left\lfloor \frac{n}{p} \right\rfloor + \left\lfloor \frac{n}{p^2} \right\rfloor + \left\lfloor \frac{n}{p^3} \right\rfloor + \left\lfloor \frac{n}{p^4} \right\rfloor + \cdots \left(p^k \le n \right)$$

Example

For any positive integer n, let $E_3(n)$ denote the index of highest power of 3 which divides $n!$. Find the value of $E_3(100)$.

Solution)

$$E_3(100) = \left\lfloor \frac{100}{3} \right\rfloor + \left\lfloor \frac{100}{3^2} \right\rfloor + \left\lfloor \frac{100}{3^3} \right\rfloor + \left\lfloor \frac{100}{3^4} \right\rfloor = 33 + 11 + 3 + 1 = 48$$

PRACTICE

1. What is the largest n such that 3^n divides 100!?

   (A) 33   (B) 44   (C) 47   (D) 48   (E) 50

2. What is the largest n such that 10^n divides 100! ?

   (A) 20   (B) 24   (C) 44   (D) 48   (E) 50

3. Let n be a positive integer greater than 4 such that the decimal representation of $n!$ ends in k zeros and the decimal representation of $(2n)!$ ends in $3k$ zeros. Let s denote the sum of the four least possible values of n. What is the sum of the digits of s ? (2015 AMC 10B #23)

   (A) 7   (B) 8   (C) 9   (D) 10   (E) 11

4. The prime factorization of 30! can be expressed in $2^a 3^b 5^c \cdots$. What is the value of $a+b+c$?

   (A) 45   (B) 46   (C) 47   (D) 48   (E) 49

5. Find the prime factorization of 15!

6. What is the largest n such that 30^n divides 100!?

35	Stars and Bars

The stars and bars method is introduced specifically to prove the following two theorems of elementary combinatorics.

Theorem one (Pairs in positive integers)

For any pair of positive integers n and k,

the number of k-tuples of **positive** integers whose sum is n

is equal to the number of $\binom{n-1}{k-1}$.

Example:

When $n = 4$ and $k = 2$, the tuples counted by the theorem are $(3,1),(2,2)$, and $(1,3)$.

there are $\binom{4-1}{2-1} = 3$ of them.

Theorem two (Pairs in non-negative integers)

For any pair of positive integers n and k,

the number of k-tuples of **non-negative** integers whose sum is n

is equal to the number of $\binom{n+k-1}{k-1}$ or $\binom{n+k-1}{n}$.

Note: $\binom{n+k-1}{k-1} = \binom{n+k-1}{n}$

Example:

When $n = 4$ and $k = 2$, the tuples counted by the theorem are

$(0,4),(1,3),(2,2),(3,1)$, and $(4,0)$.

There are $\binom{4+1}{2-1} = 5$ of them.

PRACTICE

1. Peter want to buy 8 donuts all of which are either glazed, double chocolate, or powdered donuts. In how many ways can he make the choice?

2. What is the number of solutions in <u>nonnegative integers</u> of $x_1 + x_2 + x_3 + \cdots + x_{20} = 100$?

3. How many ways to buy 10 dogs if there are 6 varieties to choose from?

4. How many nonnegative integer solutions are there to $x_1 + x_2 + x_3 \leq 10$?

5. What is the number of solutions in <u>positive integers</u> of $x_1 + x_2 + x_3 + \cdots + x_{20} = 100$? (Compare with question 2)

6. Seven <u>distinct</u> pieces of candy are to be distributed among three bags. The red bag and the blue bag must each receive at least one piece of candy; the white bag may remain empty. How many arrangements are possible? (2010 AMC 10B #22) (Compare with question #8.)

   (A) 1930   (B) 1931   (C) 1932   (D) 1933   (E) 1934

7. Alice has 24 apples. In how many ways can she share them with Becky and Chris so that each of the three people has at least two apples? (2019 AMC 8 #25)

   (A) 105   (B) 114   (C) 190   (D) 210   (E) 380

8. Thirty apples are to be distributed among five bags. The red bag and the blue bags must each receive at least three apples; the white, the green, and the yellow bag may remain empty. How many arrangements are possible?

9. A dog trainer want to buy 10 dogs all of which are either poodle, German shepherd, and golden retriever. In how many ways can he make the choice?

   (A) 50   (B) 66   (C) 120   (D) 240   (E) 286

10. Twelve apples are to be distributed among four bags. If all of the bags must receive at least one apple, how many arrangements are possible?

    (A) 56   (B) 165   (C) 220   (D) 455   (D) 480

36 | How to distribute distinct things into different rooms

Question:
Three distinct pieces of candy are to be distributed among three bags. the bags may remain empty.

Solution) You cannot apply <u>stars and bars</u> to this question, because the candies are not identical. You need to approach in different ways as follows. You assign bags (A, B, C) to the candies (c_1, c_2, c_3).

c_1	c_2	c_3
A	A	A
B	B	B
C	C	C

1. (A, A, A) means → All candies go in bag A, but the bag B and bag C are empty.

2. (A, B, B) means → Candy c_1 goes in bag A and c_2, c_3 go in bag B.

Therefore, when you consider all the bags may be remained empty, the number of arrangements is $3 \times 3 \times 3 = 27$.

If the bag A and the bag B each must receive at least one piece of candy, and the bag C may remain empty, you subtract the number of distributions with the empty bag from 27.

Case 1) Bag A is empty. The number of arrangements is $2 \times 2 \times 2 = 8$.

c_1	c_2	c_3
B	B	B
C	C	C

Case 2) Bag B is empty. The number of arrangements is $2 \times 2 \times 2 = 8$.

c_1	c_2	c_3
A	A	A
C	C	C

Note: Both of two calculations include the number with both two bags are empty. Therefore, the total overcount is $8 + 8 - 1 = 15$. The final number is $27 - 15 = 12$.

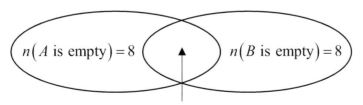

$n(\text{Both } A \text{ and } B \text{ are empty}) = 1$

PRACTICE

1. Seven distinct candies are to be distributed into three bags. If all three bags may be remained empty, how many arrangements are possible?

   (A) $_7C_3$ (B) $_{10}C_2$ (C) 7^3 (D) 3^7 (E) $_7P_3$

2. Seven distinct candies are to be distributed into three bags. If the red bag must receive at least one piece of candy, and the blue and white bags may be remained empty, how many arrangements are possible?

   (A) $_7C_3$ (B) $_7P_3$ (C) 2059   (D) 2060   (E) 2178

3. Seven distinct pieces of candy are to be distributed among three bags. The red bag and the blue bag must each receive at least one piece of candy; the white bag may remain empty. How many arrangements are possible? (2010 AMC 10B #22)

   (A) 1930   (B) 1931   (C) 1932   (D) 1933   (E) 1934

<table>
<tr><td>**37**</td><td># Pigeonhole Principle</td></tr>
</table>

In mathematics, the pigeonhole principle states that if n items are put into m containers, with $n > m$ then at least one container must contain more than one item.

Pigeonhole Principle can be used to find number to guarantee as follows.

Question

A drawer contains 8 red socks, 5 white socks, and 10 black socks. If socks are randomly taken from the drawer without replacement, how many must be taken to be sure that 7 socks of the same color have been taken?

Solution
By the Pigeon Principle, by taking 18, we make sure that we have at least 7 of the same color.

r	w	b
r	w	b
r	w	b
r	w	b
r	w	b
r		b

$\boxed{18}$

Remember: Consider the worst-case scenario! (Every time, we take different colored socks.)

PRACTICE

1. A drawer contains 12 blue socks, 8 red socks, and 9 green socks. If socks are randomly taken from the drawer without replacement, how many socks must be taken from the drawer to ensure that 4 green socks are drawn?

2. A drawer contains 12 blue socks, 8 red socks, and 9 green socks. If socks are randomly taken from the drawer without replacement, how many socks must be taken from the drawer to ensure that 3 socks of the same color have been drawn?

3. A drawer contains 12 blue socks, 8 red socks, and 9 green socks. If socks are randomly taken from the drawer without replacement, how many socks must be taken from the drawer to ensure that 3 of every colored sock have been drawn?

4. If there is an infinite number of red, blue, yellow, and black socks in a drawer, how many socks must be pulled out of the drawer to guarantee he has a pair?

5. Six distinct positive integers are randomly chosen between 1 and 2006, inclusive. What is the probability that some pair of these integers has a difference that is a multiple of 5?
(2006 AMC 10A #20)

(A) $\frac{1}{2}$ (B) $\frac{3}{5}$ (C) $\frac{2}{3}$ (D) $\frac{4}{5}$ (E) 1

6. There are 52 people in a room. What is the largest value of n such that the statement " At least n people in this room have birthdays falling in the same month" is always true?
(2011 AMC 10B #11)

(A) 2   (B) 3   (C) 4   (D) 5   (E) 12

38	How many squares does contain diagonal?

Case 1: 2×5

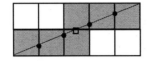

Intersections with vertical lines $= 4$ and

Intersections with horizontal lines $= 1$ except end points.

Number of squares crossed by diagonal is

$$(4+1)+1=6$$

Case 2: 4×6

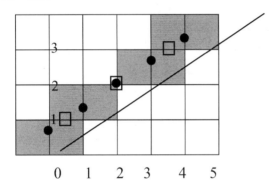

Intersections with vertical lines $= 5$ and

Intersections with horizontal lines $= 3$ except end points.

Overlapped Intersection $= 1$

Number of squares crossed by diagonal is

$$(5+3-1)+1=8$$

Algebraically, the equation of the diagonal is $y = \dfrac{2}{3}x$, where $x = 1, 2, 3, 4, 5$.

At $x = 3$, $y = 2$ means "It is an overlapped point." Therefore, total intersection is

$5+3-1=7$. Number of squares crossed by the diagonal is $7+1=8$.

Note: The number of squares crossed by diagonal = (number of intersections with vertical and horizontal lines − number of common intersections) + 1

PRACTICE

1. A rectangular floor that is 10 feet wide and 17 feet long is tiled with 170 one-foot square tiles. A bug walks from one corner to the opposite corner in a straight line. Including the first and the last tile, how many tiles does the bug visit? (2019 AMC 12A #10)

   (A) 17   (B) 25   (C) 26   (D) 27   (E) 28

2. A rectangle that is 12 feet wide and 18 feet long contain 216 squares. A diagonal is drawn from one corner to the opposite corner in a straight line. How many squares are crossed by the diagonal?

   (A) 24   (B) 25   (C) 26   (D) 27   (E) 28

39 | How to check if a number is prime

Prime numbers are always before and after multiples of 6.

5	6	7	→ 5 and 7 are prime numbers.
11	12	13	→ 11 and 13 are prime numbers.
17	18	19	→ 17 and 19 are prime numbers.
23	24	25	→ 25 is not prime, and 23 is prime.
	⋮		
1295	1296	1297	→ 1295 is not prime, and 1297 is prime

Example: Find out whether 337 is a prime number or not?

Solution) We know that 336 is a multiple of 6.

335 336 337 → 335 is not a prime number, so 337 must be a prime number.

Remember: Both two numbers before and after multiple of 6 are not always primes.

PRACTICE

1. Using the digits 1, 2, 3, 4, 5, 6, 7, and 9, form 4 two-digit prime numbers, using each digit only once. What is the sum of the 4 prime numbers? (2002 AMC 10A #15)

   (A) 150   (B) 160   (C) 170   (D) 180   (E) 190

2. Which of the following expressions is never a prime number when p is a prime number? (2018 AMC 10B #11)

   (A) $p^2 + 16$ (B) $p^2 + 24$ (C) $p^2 + 26$ (D) $p^2 + 46$ (E) $p^2 + 96$

40	Base Number

A. A numeral is a representation of a number. When we have 235,

Base 10 system: $235_{10} = 2 \cdot 10^2 + 3 \cdot 10^1 + 5 \cdot 10^0$

Base 9 system: $235_9 = 2 \cdot 9^2 + 3 \cdot 9^1 + 5 \cdot 9^0$

Base 8 system: $235_8 = 2 \cdot 8^2 + 3 \cdot 8^1 + 5 \cdot 8^0$

Base 7 system: $235_7 = 2 \cdot 7^2 + 3 \cdot 7^1 + 5 \cdot 7^0 = 124$

B. How to convert 124 to base 7?

$124 \div 7 = 17R5 \quad \rightarrow \quad 5$
$17 \div 7 = 2R3 \quad \rightarrow \quad 3$
$2 \div 7 = 0R2 \quad \rightarrow \quad 2$

Therefore, $124 = 235_7$

C. The list of digits commonly used for base 16:

$$1, \ 2, \ 3, \ 4, \ 5, \ 6, \ 7, \ 8, \ 9, \ A, \ B, \ C, \ D, \ E, \ F$$

$$\left(A = 10, \ B = 11, \ C = 12, \ D = 13, \ E = 14, \ F = 15 \right)$$

D. How to convert base b number to base b^2 number?

Example

$$211211_3 = 21_3 \quad 12_3 \quad 11_3 = \boxed{2(3)+1}\boxed{1(3)+2}\boxed{1(3)+1} = 754_9$$

PRACTICE

1. Convert 542_8 to base 10.

2. Convert 785_{10} to base 6.

3. Convert 204_6 to base 8.

4. Convert 12221122_3 to base 9.

5. The number 10! when written in the base 12 system, ends with how many zeros? (AHSME)

6. The number 8!, when written in the base 8 system, ends with how many zeros?

7. The base 3 representation of x is 121122111122211112222. Find the first digit (on the left) of the base 9 representation of x?

8. The numeral 47 in base a represents the same number as 74 in base b. Assuming that both bases are positive integers, find the least possible value for $a+b$ and leave your answer in base 10. (AHSME)

9. A number N has three digits when expressed in base 7. When N is expressed in base 9, the digits are reversed. Find the middle digit in either representation of N. (AHSME)

10. In base 10, a number N has three digits when expressed in base 4 and also three digits in base 7. How many numbers of N are there in base 10?

11. In base 10, the number 2013 ends in the digit 3. In base 9, on the other hand, the same number is written as $(2676)_9$ and ends in the digit 6. For how many positive integers b does the base-b-representation of 2013 end in the digit 3? (2013 AMC 10A #19)

    (A) 6   (B) 9   (C) 13   (D) 16   (E) 18

12. Hexadecimal (base-16) numbers are written using numeric digits 0 through 9 as well as the letters A through F to represent 10 through 15. Among the first 1000 positive integers, there are n whose hexadecimal representation contains only numeric digits. What is the sum of the digits of n? (2015 AMC 10A #18)

    (A) 17   (B) 18   (C) 19   (D) 20   (E) 21

13. A base-10 three-digit number n is selected at random. Which of the following is closest to the probability that the base-9 representation and the base-11 representation of n are both three-digit numerals? (2003 AMC 10 #20)

    (A) 0.3   (B) 0.4   (C) 0.5   (D) 0.6   (E) 0.7

Every repeating decimal number can be expresses in fraction (rational number).

Example 1

When $x = 0.\overline{3}$, then $10x = 3.\overline{3}$ and $10x - x = 3 \rightarrow (10-1)x = 3 \rightarrow x = \dfrac{3}{10-1}$

$$x = 0.\overline{3} = \frac{3}{10-1} = \frac{3}{9} \text{ or } \frac{1}{3}$$

Alternate method using infinite geometric series

$$0.\overline{3} = 3(10^{-1}) + 3(10^{-2}) + 3(10^{-3}) + \cdots = \frac{3(10^{-1})}{1-10^{-1}} = \frac{3/10}{9/10} = \frac{1}{3}$$

Example 2

1) $0.\overline{31} = \dfrac{31}{10^2 - 1} = \dfrac{31}{99}$

2) $0.\overline{301} = \dfrac{301}{10^3 - 1} = \dfrac{301}{999}$

3) $0.\overline{3}_5 = \dfrac{3_5}{5-1} = \dfrac{3}{4}$

4) $0.\overline{31}_5 = \dfrac{31_5}{5^2 - 1} = \dfrac{3(5)+1}{25-1} = \dfrac{16}{24} = \dfrac{2}{3}$

Example 3   Generally, for three repeating decimals

$$0.\overline{abc}_k = \frac{abc_k}{k^3 - 1} = \frac{a(k^2) + b(k) + c}{k^3 - 1}$$

PRACTICE

1. What is the value of $0.\overline{5}_7 = 0.5555\cdots_7$?

   (A) $\dfrac{5}{6}$ (B) $\dfrac{6}{7}$ (C) $\dfrac{5}{9}$ (D) $\dfrac{7}{10}$ (E) $\dfrac{1}{2}$

2. What is the value of $0.\overline{324}_5$?

   (A) $\dfrac{324}{555}$ (B) $\dfrac{324}{999}$ (C) $\dfrac{101}{125}$ (D) $\dfrac{101}{124}$ (E) $\dfrac{89}{124}$

3. What is the value of $0.00\overline{31}_5$?

4. What is the value of $0.0\overline{301}_4$?

5. For some positive integer k, the repeating base-k representation of the (base-ten) fraction $\frac{7}{51}$ is $0.\overline{23}_k = 0.232323\cdots_k$. What is k? (2019 AMC 10A #18, AMC 12A #12)

(A) 13   (B) 14   (C) 15   (D) 16   (E) 17

6. For some value of k, the repeating base-k representation of (base-ten) fraction $\frac{1}{10}$ is $\frac{1}{10} = 0.\overline{03}_k$. What is the value of k?

(A) 4   (B) 5   (C) 6   (D) 7   (E) 8

42   Divisibility Rules

A **divisibility rules** help us to determine whether a positive integer can be evenly divided by another A positive integer N is divisible by

Divisible by	Definition	example
2	If the last digit of N is 2, 4, 6, 8, or 0	2,458 8 is divisible by 2
3	If the sum of digits of N is a multiple of 3	$123, 1 + 2 + 3 = 6$ 6 is divisible by 3
4	If the last 2 digits of N are a multiple of 4	4,524 24 is divisible by 4
5	If the last digit of N is either 0 or 5	12,390 or 3,475 both 0 and 5 are divisible by 5
6	If N is divisible by both 2 and 3	24 24 is divisible by both 2 and 3
7	If subtracting twice the last digit of N from the remaining digits gives a multiple of 7	672 $2 + 2 = 4$, $67 - 4 = 63$, 63 is divisible by 7
8	If the last 3 digits of N are a multiple of 8	1,816 816 is divisible by 8
9	If the sum of digits of N is a multiple of 9	153 $1 + 5 + 3 = 9$, 9 is divisible by 9
10	If the last digit of is 0	257,890 0 is divisible by 10
11	If the difference of the alternating sum of digits of N is a multiple of 11	2343 is divisible by 11 because $2 - 3 + 4 - 3 = 0$, which is a multiple of 11
12	If N is divisible by both 3 and 4	1,481,481,468 is divisible by 3 and 4.

PRACTICE

1. If the number $98a6$ is multiple of 3, what are the all possible values of a?

2. For what values of a and b is $12ab$ a multiple of 99?

3. The base-ten representation for 19! is $121,6T5,100,40M,832,H00,$, where T, M, and H denote digits that are not given. What is $T + M + H$? (2019 AMC 10B #14)

(A) 3   (B) 8   (C) 12   (D) 14   (E) 17

4. The six-digit number $\underline{2}\,\underline{0}\,\underline{2}\,\underline{1}\,\underline{0}\,\underline{A}$ is prime for only one digit A. What is A?
    (2021 AMC 10 A #5)

    (A) 1   (B) 3   (C) 5   (D) 7   (E) 9

Definition of **Subset:** A set consisting of elements of a given set that can be the same as the given set or smaller.

1. If Set B is a subset of a set A, then we write $B \subseteq A$.
2. By definition, the empty set $\{\ \}$ or ϕ is a subset of every set
3. A mathematical set in which every element in the set is also contained in a larger set or in an equal set
4. If a set A have n elements, the number of subsets of set A is 2^n.

$$\text{The number of subsets} = \binom{n}{0} + \binom{n}{1} + \binom{n}{2} + \binom{n}{3} + \binom{n}{4} + \cdots + \binom{n}{n} = 2^n$$

Definition of **Proper Subset:** A proper subset of a set A is a subset of A that is not equal to A.

1. The number of subsets is $2^n - 1$.

PRACTICE

1. How many subsets of $\{2,3,4,5,6,7,8\}$ contain at least one prime number?
   (2018 AMC 10B #5)

   (A) 128   (B) 192   (C) 224   (D) 240   (E) 256

2. How many subsets of $\{1,2,3,4,5,6,7,8,9,10\}$ contain elements 3,4, and 5?

   (A) 32   (B) 64   (C) 96   (D) 128   (E) 256

3. If $A = \{1,2,3,4,5,6,7,8\}$, then the number of subsets of A that contain the element 2 but not 3 is

   (A) 16   (B) 32   (C) 64   (D) 128   (E) 256

Greatest integer function is denoted by $[x]$. This means, the greatest integer less than or equal to x.

1. If x is an integer, $[x] = x$.

2. If x is a decimal number, then $[x]$ = the integral part of x.

3. The value of $[x]$ is an integer.

4. The floor function $\lfloor x \rfloor$ is also called the greatest integer function or integer value.

The floor function satisfies the following identities.

1. $\lfloor x+n \rfloor = \lfloor x \rfloor + n$, where n = integer.

   Proof: If $\lfloor x+n \rfloor = m$, then $m \le x+n < m+1$ $\rightarrow$ $m-n \le x \le m-n+1$ $\rightarrow$ $\lfloor x \rfloor = m-n$.
   Now $m = \lfloor x \rfloor + n$ $\rightarrow$ Therefore, $\lfloor x+n \rfloor = \lfloor x \rfloor + n$.

2. $x = \lfloor x \rfloor + k$, where $0 \le k < 1$ and k = decimal part of x.
   Example: If $x = 3.17$, $3.17 = \lfloor 3.17 \rfloor + 0.17$.

3. $\lfloor 2x \rfloor = \lfloor x \rfloor + \left\lfloor x + \dfrac{1}{2} \right\rfloor$

4. $\lfloor 3x \rfloor = \lfloor x \rfloor + \left\lfloor x + \dfrac{1}{3} \right\rfloor + \left\lfloor x + \dfrac{2}{3} \right\rfloor$

5. $\lfloor mx \rfloor = \lfloor x \rfloor + \left\lfloor x + \dfrac{1}{m} \right\rfloor + \left\lfloor x + \dfrac{2}{m} \right\rfloor + \cdots + \left\lfloor x + \dfrac{m-1}{m} \right\rfloor$

5. $\lfloor -x \rfloor = \begin{cases} -\lfloor x \rfloor, & \text{if } x \text{ is an integer,} \\ -\lfloor x \rfloor - 1. & \text{if otherwise.} \end{cases}$

6. $\lfloor x \rfloor$ has only one integer value.

7. $\lfloor 2x \rfloor$ has two integer values.

8. $\lfloor mx \rfloor$ has m integer values.

PRACTICE

1. Let $\lfloor x \rfloor$ denote the greatest integer less than or equal to x. How many real numbers x satisfy the equation
$$x^2 + 10,000\lfloor x \rfloor = 10,000x\ ? \quad (2018 \text{ AMC 12B } \#24)$$

   (A) 197   (B) 198   (C) 199   (D) 200   (E) 201

2. Real numbers x and y are chosen independently and uniformly at random from the interval $(0,1)$. What is the probability that $\lfloor \log_2 x \rfloor = \lfloor \log_2 y \rfloor$, where $\lfloor r \rfloor$ denotes the greatest integer less than or equal to the real number r? (2017 AMC 12B #20)

   (A) $\dfrac{1}{8}$ (B) $\dfrac{1}{6}$ (C) $\dfrac{1}{4}$ (D) $\dfrac{1}{3}$ (E) $\dfrac{1}{2}$

3. For every real number x, let $\lfloor x \rfloor$ denote the greatest integer not exceeding x, and let
$$f(x) = \lfloor x \rfloor \left(2014^{x - \lfloor x \rfloor} - 1 \right).$$
The set of all numbers x such that $1 \le x < 2014$ and $f(x) \le 1$ is a union of disjoint intervals. What is the sum of the lengths of those intervals?
(2014 AMC 12A #21)

   (A) 1   (B) $\dfrac{\log 2015}{\log 2014}$ (C) $\dfrac{\log 2014}{\log 2013}$ (D) $\dfrac{2014}{2013}$ (E) $2014^{\frac{1}{2014}}$

4. Let x be chosen at random from the interval $(0,1)$. What is the probability that
$$\lfloor \log_{10} 4x \rfloor - \lfloor \log_{10} x \rfloor = 0\ ?$$

   Here $\lfloor x \rfloor$ denotes the greatest integer that is less than or equal to x. (2006 AMC 12B #20)

   (A) $\dfrac{1}{8}$ (B) $\dfrac{3}{20}$ (C) $\dfrac{1}{6}$ (D) $\dfrac{1}{5}$ (E) $\dfrac{1}{4}$

5. The symbolism $\lfloor x \rfloor$ denotes the largest integer not exceeding x.

   For example, $\lfloor 3 \rfloor = 3$ and $\left\lfloor \dfrac{9}{2} \right\rfloor = 4$. Compute $\lfloor \sqrt{1} \rfloor + \lfloor \sqrt{2} \rfloor + \lfloor \sqrt{3} \rfloor + \cdots \lfloor \sqrt{16} \rfloor$.

   (A) 35   (B) 38   (C) 40   (D) 42   (E) 136

45	Greatest Integer Equation

First, try to eliminate the floor and solve the inequality.

Example 1

Solve for x. $\lfloor 2x - 8 \rfloor = -4$

Solution) Eliminate the floor.

$$-4 \le 2x - 8 < -3 \;\rightarrow\; 4 \le 2x < 5 \;\rightarrow\; 2 \le x < \frac{5}{2}$$

Example 2

Solve for x. $\dfrac{x}{6} = \lfloor x \rfloor$

Solution) Since $\lfloor x \rfloor$ is an integer, x should be multiples of 6. $\rightarrow x \equiv 0 \bmod 6$

Now eliminate the floor.

$$\frac{x}{6} \le x < \frac{x}{6} + 1 \;\rightarrow\; x \le 6x < x + 6 \;\rightarrow\; 0 \le x < 1.2$$

We can see that only 0 is a multiple of 6. The answer is $x = 0$.

Example 3

Solve for x. $\dfrac{x + 100}{6} = \lfloor x \rfloor$

Since $\lfloor x \rfloor$ is an integer, $x + 100$ should be multiples of 6. $\rightarrow x \equiv 2 \bmod 6$

Because, $x + 100 \equiv 0 \bmod 6 \;\rightarrow\; x + 4 \bmod 6 \equiv 0 \bmod 6 \;\rightarrow\; x \equiv 2 \bmod 6$

Now eliminate the floor.

$$\frac{x + 100}{6} \le x < \frac{x + 100}{6} + 1 \;\rightarrow\; x + 100 \le 6x < x + 100 + 6$$

$x \ge 20$ and $x < 21.2 \;\rightarrow\; 20 \le x < 21.2$

We can see only $20 \equiv 2 \bmod 6$. The answer is $x = 20$.

PRACTICE

1. Find the values of x which satisfy

$$\frac{x}{3} = \lfloor \sqrt{x} \rfloor.$$

2. How many positive integers n satisfy

$$\frac{n+1000}{70} = \lfloor \sqrt{n} \rfloor?$$

(Recall that $\lfloor x \rfloor$ is the greatest integer not exceeding x.) (2020 AMC 10B #24)

(A) 2   (B) 4   (C) 6   (D) 30   (E) 32

3. How many positive integers n satisfy

$$\frac{n+100}{50} = \lfloor \sqrt{n} \rfloor?$$

(A) 1   (B) 2   (C) 3   (D) 4   (E) 5

46	Transformation of Greatest Integer Equation

Parent function: $y = [x]$

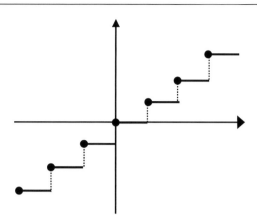

$y = [x] + 2$: Vertical shift $\rightarrow$ 2 units up

$y = [x] - 2$: Vertical shift $\rightarrow$ 2 units down

$y = [-x]$: Reflection over y-axis

$y = -[x]$: Reflection over x-axis

$y = [x - 2]$: Horizontal shift $\rightarrow$ 2 units right

$y = [x + 2]$: Horizontal shift $\rightarrow$ 2 units left

$y = 2[x]$: Vertical stretch $\rightarrow$ by factor of 2

PRACTICE

1. The graph of $f(x) = \lfloor x \rfloor - \lfloor 1 - x \rfloor$ is symmetric about which of the following? (Here $\lfloor x \rfloor$ is the greatest integer not exceeding x.) (2021 AMC 10A #16)

   (A) the y-axis   (B) the line $x = 1$ (C) the origin   (D) the point $\left(\dfrac{1}{2}, 0\right)$ (E) the point $(1, 0)$

47 | General Probability

Probability is the branch of mathematics concerning numerical descriptions of how likely an event is to occur, or how likely it is that a proposition is true. The probability of an event is a number between 0 and 1, where, roughly speaking, 0 indicates impossibility of the event and 1 indicates certainty.

$$\text{Probability} = \frac{\text{Successful outcomes}}{\text{All possible outcomes}}$$

$$\text{Expected value} = \sum_i n_i p_i$$

$$P_i = \text{The probability of the event}$$

$$n_i = \text{The number of the event}$$

PRACTICE

1. When a certain unfair die is rolled, an even number is 3 times as likely to appear as an odd number. The die is rolled twice. What is the probability that the sum of the numbers rolled is even? (2021 AMC 10A #9)

   (A) $\dfrac{3}{8}$　　(B) $\dfrac{4}{9}$　　(C) $\dfrac{5}{9}$　　(D) $\dfrac{9}{16}$　　(E) $\dfrac{5}{8}$

2. A school has 100 students and 5 teachers. In the first period, each student is taking one class, and each teacher is teaching one class. The enrollments in the classes are 50, 20, 20, 5 and 5. Let t be the average value obtained if a teacher is picked at random and the number of students in their class is noted. Let s be the average value obtained if a student was picked at random and the number of students in their class, including the student, is noted. What is $t - s$? (2021 AMC 10 A #10)

   (A) −18.5　　(B) −13.5　　(C) 0　　(D) 13.5　　(E) 18.5

3. Each of the 20 balls is tossed independently and at random into one of the 5 bins. Let p be the probability that some bin ends up with 3 balls, another with 5 balls, and the other three with 4 balls each. Let q be the probability that every bin ends up with 4 balls. What is $\dfrac{p}{q}$? (2021 AMC 10A #21)

   (A) 1　　(2) 4　　(C) 8　　(D) 12　　(E) 16

48	Geometric Probability

Geometric probability is a tool to deal with the problem of infinite outcomes by measuring the number of outcomes geometrically, in terms of length, area, or volume.

PRACTICE

1. A point (x, y) is randomly picked from inside the rectangle with vertices $(0,0),(4,0),(4,1),$ and $(0,1)$. What is the probability that $x < y$? (2003 AMC 10A #12)

   (A) $\dfrac{1}{8}$ (B) $\dfrac{1}{4}$ (C) $\dfrac{3}{8}$ (D) $\dfrac{1}{2}$ (E) $\dfrac{3}{4}$

2. If a circle with radius of 8 is inscribed in a square with a length of 16, what is the probability that a dart thrown will land inside of the square and outside of the circle?

   (A) $\dfrac{1}{12}$ (B) $\dfrac{4-\pi}{8}$ (C) $\dfrac{\pi-3}{4}$ (D) $\dfrac{\pi-4}{4}$ (E) $\dfrac{\pi}{4}$

49	**Symmetric Probability (1)**

Definition of Symmetric probability

1. If different outcomes are equivalent, they should have the same **probability**.

2. Symmetric probability refers to a situation in which multiple viewpoints will behave exactly the same.

Example

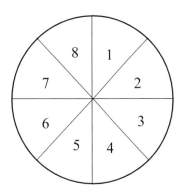

On the disk shown above, a player spins the arrow twice. The fraction a and b is formed, where a is the number of the sector where the arrow stops after the first spin and b is the number of the sector where the arrow stops after the second spin. On every spin, each of the numbered sectors has an equal probability of being the sector on which the arrow stops. What is the probability that the fraction $\dfrac{a}{b}$ is greater than 1?

Solution

There will be three outcomes

$$\begin{cases} 1.\ a > b \\ 2.\ a = b \\ 3.\ a < b \end{cases} \quad \text{and 1. and 3. should have the same probability (Symmetric probability).}$$

Total number of outcomes is $6 \times 6 = 36$ and the number of outcomes of $a = b$ is 6. It gives us

$$P(a = b) = \frac{6}{36} = \frac{1}{6}.$$

Therefore, $P(a > b) = \dfrac{1 - \dfrac{1}{6}}{2} = \dfrac{5}{12}$.

PRACTICE

1. Two players Anton and Bishop cast a die numbered 1 to 6. What is the probability that Anton's number is greater than Bishop's number?

(A) $\dfrac{1}{6}$ (B) $\dfrac{5}{12}$ (C) $\dfrac{1}{2}$ (D) $\dfrac{2}{3}$ (E) $\dfrac{5}{6}$

2. Bernardo randomly picks 3 distinct numbers from the set $\{1,2,3,4,5,6,7,8,9\}$ and arranges them in descending order to form a 3-digit number. Silvia randomly picks 3 distinct numbers from the set $\{1,2,3,4,5,6,7,8\}$ and also arranges them in descending order to form a 3-digit number. What is the probability that Bernardo's number is larger than Silvia's number?
(2010 AMC 10A #18)

(A) $\dfrac{47}{72}$ (B) $\dfrac{37}{56}$ (C) $\dfrac{2}{3}$ (D) $\dfrac{49}{72}$ (E) $\dfrac{39}{56}$

3. A red ball and a green ball are randomly and independently tossed into bins numbered with positive integers so that for each ball, the probability that it is tossed into bin k is 2^{-k} for $k = 1,2,3,4\cdots$. What is the probability that the red ball is tossed into a higher-numbered bin than the green ball? (2019 AMC 10B #17, 12B #13)

(A) $\dfrac{1}{4}$ (B) $\dfrac{2}{7}$ (C) $\dfrac{1}{3}$ (D) $\dfrac{3}{8}$ (E) $\dfrac{3}{7}$

4. Two players A and B randomly picks 2 distinct numbers from the set $\{1,2,3,4,5,6,7,8,9,10\}$ and arranges in descending order to form a 2-digit number. What is the probability that player A's number is less than player B's number?

(A) $\dfrac{1}{5}$ (B) $\dfrac{4}{9}$ (C) $\dfrac{7}{15}$ (D) $\dfrac{22}{45}$ (E) $\dfrac{5}{9}$

5. Ms. Carri asks her students to read any 5 of the 10 books on a reading list. Harold randomly selects 5 books from this list, and Betty does the same. What is the probability that there are exactly 2 books that they both select ? (2020 AMC 10B #11)

(A) $\dfrac{1}{8}$ (B) $\dfrac{5}{36}$ (C) $\dfrac{14}{45}$ (D) $\dfrac{25}{63}$ (E) $\dfrac{1}{2}$

50	Symmetric Probability (2)

Geometric Probability

Consider the following figure to find probability.

Case 1) Imagine that there is a boat floating down the stream by a great storm.

What is the probability that the boat can reach shore A?

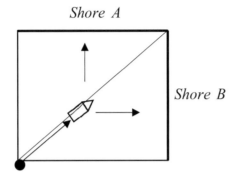

Shore A

Shore B

Solution)

Since the boat is in the equidistance from both two shores, the chance it will hit the shore A is $\frac{1}{2}$.

PRACTICE

1. A frog sitting at the point $(1,2)$ begins a sequence of jumps, where each jump is parallel to one of the coordinate axes and has length 1, and the direction of each jump (up, down, right, or left) is chosen independently at random. The sequence ends when the frog reaches a side of the square with vertices $(0,0)$, $(0,4)$,$(4,4)$ and $(4,0)$. What is the probability that the sequence of jumps ends on a vertical side of the square? (2020 AMC 10A #13)?

(A) $\frac{1}{2}$ (B) $\frac{5}{8}$ (C) $\frac{2}{3}$ (D) $\frac{3}{4}$ (E) $\frac{7}{8}$

51	Logarithm

Log Operation: $(b > 0 \text{ and } b \neq 1)$

1) $\log_b 1 = 0$	8) $\log_B A = \dfrac{\log_b A}{\log_b B}$ (Change of Base)
2) $\log_b b = 1$	9) $\log_b a = \dfrac{1}{\log_a b}$ (Reciprocal)
3) $\log_{10} a = \log a$ (Common Log)	10) $\log_a b = \log_{a^n} b^n$
4) $\log_e a = \ln a$ (Natural Log)	Example: $\log_2 5 = \log_{2^3} 5^3 = \log_8 125$
5) $\log_b (A \cdot B) = \log_b A + \log_b B$	$\log_2 5 = \log_{\sqrt{2}} \sqrt{5}$
6) $\log_b \left(\dfrac{A}{B}\right) = \log_b A - \log_b B$	11) $b^{\log_b A} = A$
7) $\log_b A^k = k \log_b A$ (Power rule)	12) $e^{\ln A} = A$

PRACTICE

1. Let S be the set of ordered triples (x, y, z) of real numbers for which

$$\log_{10}(x+y) = z \quad \text{and} \quad \log_{10}(x^2 + y^2) = z + 1$$

There are real numbers a and b such that for all ordered triples (x, y, z) in S we have $x^3 + y^3 = a \cdot 10^{3z} + b \cdot 10^{2x}$. What is the value of $a + b$? (2005 AMC 12B #23)

(A) $\dfrac{15}{2}$ (B) $\dfrac{29}{2}$ (C) 15   (D) $\dfrac{39}{2}$ (E) 24

2. How many ordered triples of integers (a, b, c) with $a \geq 2$, $b \geq 1$, and $c \geq 0$, satisfy both $\log_a b = c^{2005}$ and $a + b + c = 2005$? (2005 AMC 12A #21)

(A) 0   (B) 1   (C) 2   (D) 3   (E) 4

3. How many distinct four-tuples (a,b,c,d) of national numbers are there with

$$a \log_{10} 2 + b \log_{10} 3 + c \log_{10} 5 + d \log_{10} 7 = 2005 ?\qquad \text{(2005 AMC 12B \#17)}$$

(A) 0   (B) 1   (C) 17   (D) 2004   (E) Infinitely many

4. Let

$$S_1 = \left\{ (x,y) \mid \log_{10}\left(1 + x^2 + y^2\right) \le 1 + \log_{10}(x+y) \right\}$$

and

$$S_2 = \left\{ (x,y) \mid \log_{10}\left(2 + x^2 + y^2\right) \le 2 + \log_{10}(x+y) \right\}$$

What is the ratio of the area of S_2 to the area of S_1? (2006 AMC 12A \#21)

(A) 98   (B) 99   (C) 100   (D) 101   (E) 102

5. A circle has a radius of $\log_{10}\left(a^2\right)$ and a circumference of $\log_{10}\left(b^4\right)$. What is $\log_a b$? (2008 AMC 12B \#14)

(A) $\dfrac{1}{4\pi}$ (B) $\dfrac{1}{\pi}$ (C) π (D) 2π (E) $10^{2\pi}$

6. For what value of x does

$$\log_{\sqrt{2}} \sqrt{x} + \log_2 x + \log_4 x^2 + \log_8 x^3 + \log_{16} x^4 = 40 ?\qquad \text{(2010 AMC 12B \#12)}$$

(A) 8   (B) 16   (C) 32   (D) 256   (E) 1024

52	Factoring $x^{2n+1} - 1$ and $x^{2n+1} + 1$

A) Factoring $x^{2n+1} + 1$

Remember: If $P(x) = x^{2n+1} + 1$, then $P(-1) = 0$. $(n = 1, 2, 3, \cdots)$

$P(x)$ has a factor of $(x+1)$.

By using the synthetic division,

1) $x^3 + 1 = (x+1)(x^2 - x + 1)$

2) $x^5 + 1 = (x+1)(x^4 - x^3 + x^2 - x + 1)$

3) $x^7 + 1 = (x+1)(x^6 - x^5 + x^4 - x^3 + x^2 - x + 1)$

$\vdots$

4) $x^{17} + 1 = (x+1)(x^{16} - x^{15} + x^{14} - x^{13} + \cdots - x + 1)$

By synthetic division, you can the signs vary alternately.

$$
\begin{array}{r|cccccccccccccccccc}
-1 & 1 & 0 & 0 & 0 & 0 & 0 & 0 & 0 & 0 & 0 & 0 & 0 & 0 & 0 & 0 & 0 & 0 & 1 \\
   &   & -1 & 1 & -1 & 1 & -1 & 1 & -1 & 1 & -1 & 1 & -1 & 1 & -1 & 1 & -1 & 1 & -1 \\
\hline
   & 1 & -1 & 1 & -1 & 1 & -1 & 1 & -1 & 1 & -1 & 1 & -1 & 1 & -1 & 1 & -1 & 1 & 0
\end{array}
$$

B) Factoring $x^{2n+1} - 1$

Remember: If $P(x) = x^{2n+1} - 1$, then $P(1) = 0$. $(n = 1, 2, 3, \cdots)$

$P(x)$ has a factor of $(x-1)$.

By using the synthetic division,

1) $x^3 - 1 = (x-1)(x^2 + x + 1)$

2) $x^5 - 1 = (x-1)(x^4 + x^3 + x^2 + x + 1)$

3) $x^7 - 1 = (x-1)(x^6 + x^5 + x^4 + x^3 + x^2 + x + 1)$

$\vdots$

$\vdots$

4) $x^{17} - 1 = (x-1)(x^{16} + x^{15} + x^{14} + x^{13} + \cdots + x + 1)$

By synthetic division, you can the signs are all $(+)$.

1	1	0	0	0	0	0	0	0	0	0	0	0	0	0	0	0	0	−1
		1	1	1	1	1	1	1	1	1	1	1	1	1	1	1	1	1
	1	1	1	1	1	1	1	1	1	1	1	1	1	1	1	1	1	0

PRACTICE

1. There exists a unique strictly increasing sequence of nonnegative

   integers $a_1 < a_2 < \cdots < a_k$ such that

   $$\frac{2^{289}+1}{2^{17}+1} = 2^{a_1} + 2^{a_2} + \cdots + 2^{a_k}.$$

   What is k? (2020 AMC 10 #21)

   (A) 117   (B) 136   (C) 137   (D) 273   (E) 306

2. What is the greatest power of 2 that is a factor of $10^{1002} - 4^{501}$? (2014 AMC 10B #17)

   (A) 2^{1002} (B) 2^{1003} (C) 2^{1004} (D) 2^{1005} (E) 2^{1006}

Given a number N and number of terms k,

Case 1) If $k = $ odd, and the median is m, then $mk = N$.

    If $N = 15$, then $mk = 15$. Possible values of m and k are as follows.

$$\square\square\square\cdots\boxed{m}\cdots\square\square\square$$

  $m = $ factors of $15 = 5, 3, 1$ ($m \neq 15$)

m	k	Representations
5	3	$4 + \boxed{5} + 6$
3	5	$1 + 2 + \boxed{3} + 4 + 5$
1	15	$(-6) + (-5) + \cdots + 0 + \boxed{1} + \cdots + 6 + 7 + 8$ Some of numbers are not positive.

    There are only two ways.

Case 2) If $k = $ even, and the median is $\dfrac{m + (m+1)}{2} = \dfrac{2m+1}{2}$, then $\dfrac{(2m+1)k}{2} = N$.

    If $N = 15$, then $(2m+1)k = 30$. Factors of $30 = 1, 2, 3, 5, 6, 10, 15$

    Therefore, $2m + 1 = 1, 3, 5, 15 \;\rightarrow\; m = 0, 1, 2, 7$

$$\square\square\square\cdots\boxed{m}\boxed{m+1}\cdots\square\square\square$$

$2m+1$	$k = $ even	Representations
15	2	$7 + 8$
5	6	$0 + 1 + 2 + 3 + 4 + 5$ (0 is not positive number. We already have it in case 1)
3	10	$(-3) + (-2) + (-1) + 0 + 1 + 2 + 3 + 4 + 5 + 6$ (Some of numbers are not positive.)

    There is only one way.

    Therefore, there are three ways to represent 15 as a sum of two or more consecutive
Positive numbers.

PRACTICE

1. In how many ways can a number 65 be expressed as a sum of two or more consecutive positive numbers?

2. The sum of some positive consecutive integers is 2012. Find the smallest of these integers. (Awesome Math)

3. In how many ways can 345 be written as the sum of an increasing sequence of two or more consecutive positive integers? (2016 AMC 10B #18)

    (A) 1   (B) 3   (C) 5   (D) 6   (E) 7

4. If the sum of some positive consecutive integers is 483, what is the smallest of these integers?

    (A) 2   (B) 5   (C) 8   (D) 10   (E) 28

| **54** | Abraham de Moivre's Formula |

Every complex number can be written in the form $r(\cos\theta + i\sin\theta)$ for $r \geq 0$ and θ.

Polar form: $r(\cos\theta + i\sin\theta)$

Exponential form: e^{ix}

Cis form: $cis\theta$

In mathematics, de Moivre's formula (also known as de Moivre's theorem and de Moivre's identity) states that for any real number x and integer n it holds that

$$\left[r(\cos x + i\sin x)\right]^n = r^n(\cos nx + i\sin nx)$$

where i is the imaginary unit ($i^2 = -1$).

The expression $\cos x + i\sin x$ is sometimes abbreviated to cis x.

$$\cos x + i\sin x = cis\,x$$

Euler's formula (Exponential form)

$$e^{ix} = \cos x + i\sin x, \quad e^{-ix} = \cos(-x) + i\sin(-x) = \cos x - i\sin x$$

$$\cos x = \frac{e^{ix} + e^{-ix}}{2}, \quad \sin x = \frac{e^{ix} - e^{-ix}}{2i}$$

These can be used to give explicit expressions for the nth roots of unity, that is, complex numbers z such that $z^n = 1$.

Properties of nth roots of unity $z^n = 1$ and $n = \text{even}$

    1. Sum of all nth roots is 0.

    2. Sum of all nth roots except $z^0 = -1$

    3. Product of all roots $= -1$ $(n = \text{even})$, Product of all roots $= 1$ $(n = \text{odd})$

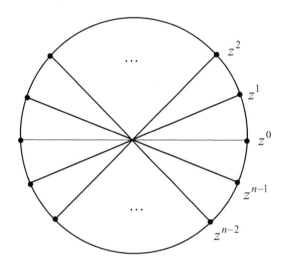

    3. z^k and z^{n-k} are conjugate roots. z^1 and z^{n-1} are conjugate roots.

    4. $\left(z^a\right)\left(z^b\right) = z^{a+b}$, $\left(z^2\right)\left(z^5\right) = z^7$

Example 1: Find the value of $\left(-\dfrac{1}{2} + \dfrac{\sqrt{3}}{2} i\right)^{99}$.

    Step 1) Express in polar form.

$$-\frac{1}{2} + \frac{\sqrt{3}}{2} i = \cos\frac{2\pi}{3} + i\sin\frac{2\pi}{3}$$

    Step 2) Apply de Moivre's formula.

$$\left(\cos\frac{2\pi}{3} + i\sin\frac{2\pi}{3}\right)^{99} = \cos 99\left(\frac{2\pi}{3}\right) + i\sin 99\left(\frac{2\pi}{3}\right) = \cos\left(66\pi\right) + i\sin\left(66\pi\right)$$

$$= \cos 0 + i\sin 0 = 1$$

Example 2: If $z = 3\left(\cos\theta + i\sin\theta\right)$, what is the $|z|$ in terms of r and θ?

$$z = 3\cos\theta + i3\sin\theta \;\rightarrow\; |z| = \sqrt{\left(3\cos\theta\right)^2 + \left(3\sin\theta\right)^2} = 3$$

Example 3: Write $3 - i\sqrt{3}$ in exponential form.

$$r = |z| = \sqrt{3^2 + \left(-\sqrt{3}\right)^2} = 2\sqrt{3}$$

$$z = 2\sqrt{3}\left(\frac{\sqrt{3}}{2} - i\frac{1}{2}\right) = 2\sqrt{3}\left(\cos\frac{11\pi}{6} + i\sin\frac{11\pi}{6}\right) = 2\sqrt{3}e^{i\left(\frac{11\pi}{6}\right)}$$

PRACTICE

1. Write each of the following in polar form.

   (a) $2 - 2i$ (b) $-6i$ (c) $-1 + i$

2. Write each of the following in rectangular form.

   (a) $6\, cis\, 120°$ (b) $e^{i\frac{\pi}{3}}$ (c) $9\, cis\, \frac{3\pi}{4}$

3. Express each of the following in exponential form.

   (a) $1 - i$ (b) $\frac{1}{2} - \frac{\sqrt{3}}{2}i$ (c) $-3i$

4. Prove $z\bar{z} = |z|^2$.

5. Find the positive integer n such that

$$\arctan\frac{1}{3} + \arctan\frac{1}{4} + \arctan\frac{1}{5} + \arctan\frac{1}{n} = \frac{\pi}{4}$$

   (AIME)

55	Roots of $f(x) = x^n - 1$

The roots of $f(x) = x^n - 1$, $n > 1$, are called the nth roots of unity.

Example 1:

The roots of $f(x) = x^3 - 1$ are $e^{i0}, e^{i\frac{2\pi}{3}}, e^{i\frac{4\pi}{3}}$.

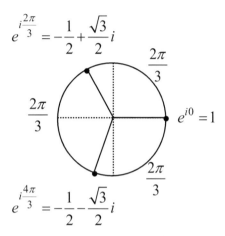

$$e^{i\frac{2\pi}{3}} = -\frac{1}{2} + \frac{\sqrt{3}}{2}i$$

$$e^{i0} = 1$$

$$e^{i\frac{4\pi}{3}} = -\frac{1}{2} - \frac{\sqrt{3}}{2}i$$

Angle between the roots is $\dfrac{2\pi}{3}$.

Example 2:

The roots of $f(x) = x^4 - 1$ are $e^{i0}, e^{i\frac{2\pi}{4}}, e^{i\frac{4\pi}{4}}, e^{i\frac{6\pi}{4}} \rightarrow 1, i, -1, -i$.

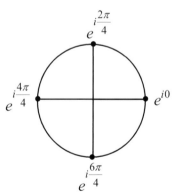

Angle between the roots is $\dfrac{2\pi}{4} = \dfrac{\pi}{2}$.

Example 3:

The roots of $f(x) = x^5 - 1$ are $e^{i0}, e^{i\frac{2\pi}{5}}, e^{i\frac{4\pi}{5}}, e^{i\frac{6\pi}{5}}, e^{i\frac{8\pi}{5}}$.

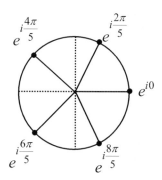

Angle between the roots is $\dfrac{2\pi}{5}$.

Properties of the roots

1) Sum of all roots $= 0$

2) If ω is a root of $x^n - 1 = 0$, then $\bar{\omega}$ is also the root of the equation.

3) If ω is a root of $x^n - 1 = 0$, then $\dfrac{1}{\omega}$ is also the root of the equation.

$$f\left(\frac{1}{\omega}\right) = \frac{1}{\omega^n} - 1 = \frac{1}{1} - 1 = 0 \text{ , because } \omega^n = 1.$$

PRACTICE

1. Find the roots of $f(x) = x^8 + x^7 + x^6 + x^5 + x^4 + x^3 + x^2 + x + 1$.

2. Find the roots of $f(x) = x^6 + x^4 + x^2 + 1$.

ANSWERS AND EXPLANATIONS

Positive divisors (Factors) using Prime Factorization

1. Prime factorization: $51^6 = 3^6 \cdot 17^6$

Perfect squares of 3^6	Perfect squares of 17^6
$3^0 = 1^2$	1^2
3^2	17^2
3^4	17^4
3^6	17^6

Therefore, the number of perfect squares is $4 \times 4 = 16$. The answer is (B).

2. Perfect cubes

Perfect cubes of 3^6	Perfect cubes of 17^6
$3^0 = 1^3$	1^3
3^3	17^3
3^6	17^6

Therefore, the number of perfect cubes is $3 \times 3 = 9$. The answer is (C).

3. Perfect squares or perfect cubes
   (Number of perfect squares $+$ number of perfect cubes) $-$ number of common
   Therefore, $(16 + 9) - 4 = 21$. The answer is (A).

Square and cube of 3^6	Square and cube of 17^6
1^6	1^6
3^6	17^6

4. $201^9 = 3^9 \times 67^9$

Perfect squares of 3^9	Perfect squares of 67^9
$3^0 = 1^2$	1^2
3^2	67^2
3^4	67^4
3^6	67^6
3^8	67^8

Perfect cubes of 3^9	Perfect cubes of 67^9
1^3	1^3
3^3	67^3
3^6	67^6
3^9	67^9

There are $5 \times 5 = 25$ perfect squares, $4 \times 4 = 16$ prefect cubes, and common is $2 \times 2 = 4$.

Therefore, there are $(25 + 16) - 4 = 37$ numbers. The answer is (C).

5. Number of positive divisors: $(9+1)(9+1) = 100$.

6. Number of factors of $21^3 = 3^3 \times 7^3$ is $(3+1)(3+1) = 16$

   The product is $21^{16/2} = 21^8$.

7. Sum of all positive divisors is $(1 + 3 + 9 + 27)(1 + 7 + 49 + 343) = 40 \times 400 = 16000$.

8. Prime factorization: $12600 = 2^3 \times 3^2 \times 5^2 \times 7^1$

   Number of factors is $(3+1)(2+1)(2+1)(1+1) = 72$.

Factors of 2^3	$\cdots$
$2^0 = 1$	
$2^1 = 2$	$\cdots$
$2^2 = 4$	
$2^3 = 8$	

You can see there are three even numbers in the factors of 2^3, and even number $\times$ any integer is also even. Therefore, probability is $\dfrac{3}{4}$.

9. Remember: When we have $n = 8 = 2^3$, number of positive divisors is $(3+1) = 4$.

   Therefore, $f_1(8) = 2(4) = 8$. Continue to check: $f_2(8) = f_1(f_1(8)) = 8 \rightarrow f_j(n) = 8$

   Another number that has 4 divisors: If $n = 6$,

   $$n = 6 = 2 \times 3 \rightarrow f_1(6) = 8 \rightarrow f_1(f_1(6)) = f_1(8) = 8 \rightarrow f_j(6) = 8$$

   That implies if $f_{50}(n) = 12$, then n must be the numbers that have $\dfrac{12}{2} = 6$ divisors.

   Case 1) one prime: $p^e \rightarrow e = 5$

   $$n \rightarrow 2^5, \cancel{3^5}, \cdots n = 32 \qquad \rightarrow \text{one number}$$

   Case 2) two primes: $p_1^{e1} p_2^{e2}$

   $$2^1 \times 3^2, \ 2^1 \times 5^2, \ 2^2 \times 3^1, \ 2^2 \times 3^1, \ 2^2 \times 5^1, \ 2^2 \times 7^1, \ 2^2 \times 11^1$$

   $$3^2 \times 5^1, \qquad\qquad\qquad\qquad\qquad\qquad\qquad \rightarrow 9 \text{ numbers}$$

   $$5^2 \times 2^1$$

   Therefore, the number of possible n is $9 + 1 = 10$. The answer is (D).

1.

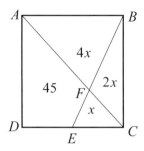

You can see $\triangle ABF \sim \triangle EFC$ with a ratio of $2:1$ and $BF:FE = 2:1$ by $CPCTC$.

Therefore, by the theorem, if the area of $\triangle EFC$ is x, the area of $\triangle BCF$ is $2x$, and the area of $\triangle ABF = 4x$. (In similar, if the ratio of the lengths is $a:b$, the ratio of the areas is $a^2:b^2$, or $AF:FC = 2:1 \rightarrow$ area of $\triangle ABF = 2 \times$ area of $\triangle BCF$)

Now you can see that $4x+2x = 45+x \rightarrow x=9$.

Therefore, the area of $ABCD = 2(45+9) = 108$. The answer is (B).

2.

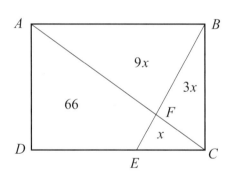

Same as question 1.

Since $\dfrac{CE}{AB} = \dfrac{1}{3}$, $\dfrac{EF}{FB} = \dfrac{1}{3}$. If $[\triangle EFC] = x$, then $[BFC] = 3x$ and $\triangle ABF = 9x$.

Therefore, $66+x = 9x+3x \rightarrow 66 = 11x \rightarrow x=6$. *$[\triangle EFC]$ stands for area.

The area of $EFC = x = 6$. The answer is (A).

3. Draw line $\overline{DF}$.

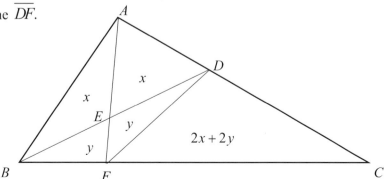

If $[AED] = x$, then $[AEB] = x$ because $BE = ED$.

If $[BEF] = y$, then $[DEF] = y$ because $BE = ED$.

If $[ADF] = x + y$, then $[CDF] = 2x + 2y$ because $AD:DC = 1:2$.

Now $\dfrac{[ABD]}{[DBC]} = \dfrac{1}{2} \rightarrow \dfrac{x+x}{y+y+2x+2y} = \dfrac{1}{2} \rightarrow \dfrac{2x}{2x+4y} = \dfrac{1}{2} \rightarrow x = 2y$, because $AD:DC = 1:2$.

Total area is $4x + 4y = 8y + 4y = 12y \rightarrow 12y = 360 \rightarrow y = 30$

The answer is (B).

4. Draw line $\overline{DF}$.

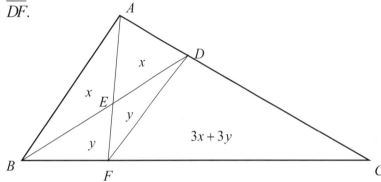

If $[AED] = x$, then $[AEB] = x$ because $BE = ED$.

If $[BEF] = y$, then $[DEF] = y$ because $BE = ED$.

If $[ADF] = x + y$, then $[CDF] = 3(x+y) = 3x + 3y$ because $AD:DC = 1:3$.

Now $\dfrac{[ABD]}{[DBC]} = \dfrac{1}{3} \rightarrow \dfrac{x+x}{y+y+3x+3y} = \dfrac{1}{3} \rightarrow \dfrac{2x}{3x+5y} = \dfrac{1}{3} \rightarrow 6x = 3x + 5y \rightarrow 3x = 5y$,

because $AD:DC = 1:3$.

Total area is $5x + 5y = 5x + 3x = 8x \rightarrow 8x = 80 \rightarrow x = 10$ and $y = 6$.

The answer is (D).

3	Triangle after two isosceles triangles built in right triangle is a right triangle

1. The figure looks as follow.

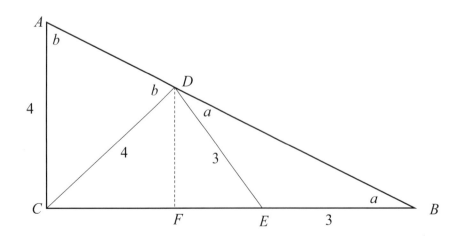

126

$\triangle ACD$ and $\triangle BDE$ are isosceles. If $\angle B = a$, then $\angle BDE = a$, $\angle A = \angle CDA = b$.

We can see $\angle CDE = 90°$ and $CE = 5$.

Now draw line DF. $\rightarrow$ $DF = \dfrac{3 \times 4}{5} = 2.4$

Since $\triangle ABC \sim \triangle DBF$, $\dfrac{4}{2.4} = \dfrac{AB}{DB} \rightarrow \dfrac{AB}{DB} = \dfrac{5}{3} \rightarrow AD = 5 - 3 = 2$.

Therefore, $\dfrac{AD}{DB} = \dfrac{2}{3}$. The answer is (A).

2.

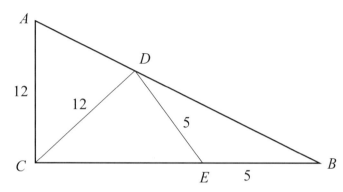

Now we know that $\triangle CDE$ is a right triangle. Therefore, the area of $\triangle CDE$ is $\dfrac{5 \times 12}{2} = 30$. The answer is (C).

3.

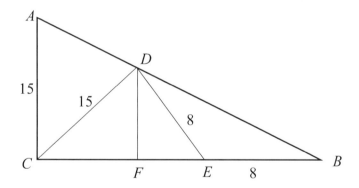

Now we know that $\triangle CDE$ is a right triangle. Therefore, $CE = \sqrt{15^2 + 8^2} = 17$.

And $DF = \dfrac{8 \times 15}{17} = \dfrac{120}{17}$.

The area of $\triangle EDB = \dfrac{EB \times DF}{2} = \dfrac{8\left(\dfrac{120}{17}\right)}{2} = \dfrac{480}{17}$. The answer is (B)

4	Right Triangle Proportion

1.

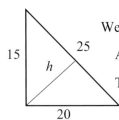

We can see that it is a right triangle with possible altitudes of $15, 20$, or h.

Area of the triangle $= \dfrac{15 \times 20}{2} = \dfrac{25 \times h}{2} \rightarrow h = 12$

Therefore, the shortest altitude is 12.   The answer is (B).

2. a) $CD^2 = 4 \times 9 \rightarrow CD = 6$ b) $BC^2 = 9(9+4) \rightarrow BC = 3\sqrt{13}$

   c) $AC^2 = 4(4+9) \rightarrow AC = 2\sqrt{13}$

3. We need to draw $\overline{BF}$, which is the height of ΔABC. We already have the area of ΔACD,

$\dfrac{20 \times 30}{2} = 300$. Now find the area of ΔABC.

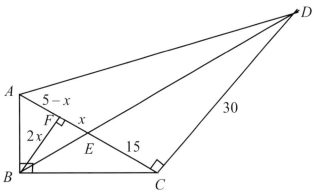

Since $\Delta AFE \sim \Delta CED$, if $FE = x$, then $BF = 2x$. $CD = 2(CE)$

Now apply the right triangle proportion. $(x+15)(5-x) = (2x)^2 \rightarrow x^2 + 2x - 15 = 0$

$(x+5)(x-3) = 0 \rightarrow x = 3$, $BF = 2(3) = 6$. Therefore, the area of $\Delta ABC = \dfrac{20 \times 6}{2} = 60$.

Total area is $300 + 60 = 360$. The answer is (D).

5	Concurrent (Angle Bisector, Median, Altitude, Perpendicular Bisector)

1. Angle bisector theorem: $\dfrac{AB}{BC} = \dfrac{3}{8} \rightarrow$ Let $AB = 3a$ and $BC = 8a$.

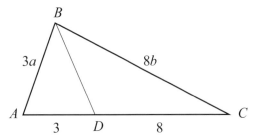

By triangle inequality, $8a - 3a < AC < 3a + 8a \rightarrow 5a < 11 < 11a$. The only integer value of a is 2.

Therefore, the perimeter is $3(2)+8(2)+11=33$. The answer is (B).

2.

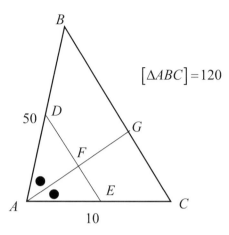

$[\triangle ABC]=120$

By angle bisector theorem, $\dfrac{BG}{EG}=\dfrac{50}{10}=\dfrac{5}{1} \rightarrow$ Area of $\triangle ABG=120\left(\dfrac{5}{6}\right)=100$

Now, $\triangle ABG \sim \triangle ADF \rightarrow$ The ratio of their lengths $=\dfrac{50}{25}=\dfrac{2}{1}$

You can see the ratio of their areas is $\dfrac{2^2}{1^2}=\dfrac{4}{1}$. Therefore, the area of $BDFG$ is $100\left(\dfrac{3}{4}\right)=75$.

The answer is (D).

| 6 | Cyclic Quadrilaterals |

1. $m\angle ABC=100$ and $m\angle BAD=\dfrac{100}{2}=50$. $m\angle BCD=180-50=130$. Therefore,

$m\angle BDC=180-(130+15)=35$

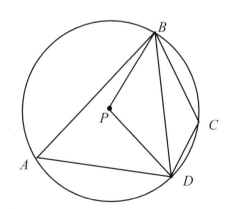

2. Since $6 \times 4 = 3 \times 8$, Quadrilateral $ABCD \frac{\pi}{2}$ is cyclic. Inscribed angles for the same arc are equal in

measure. $m\angle ABP = m\angle PCD = 40^\circ$

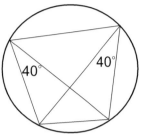

3. $\angle DBC = \angle DAC = 50$ and $\angle DAB = 50 + 60 = 110$. Therefore, $\angle BCD = 180 - 110 = 70^\circ$

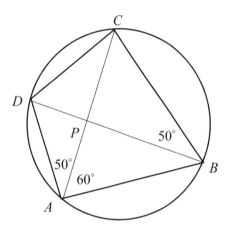

4. Since $\angle ADC$ and $\angle AEC$ are right angles, you can see $ADEC$ is a cyclic quadrilateral.
   $\angle BAE = \angle DCE = 30$ and $\angle ECA = 20 + 30 = 50$. $\angle ADE = 180 - 50 = 130$

   $\angle CDE = 130 - 90 = 40^\circ$

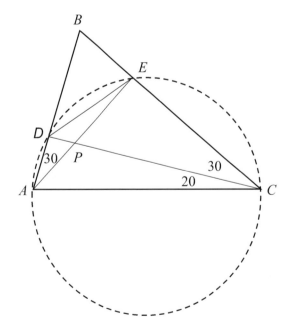

5. We can see $PW = 3$ and $WR = 4$.

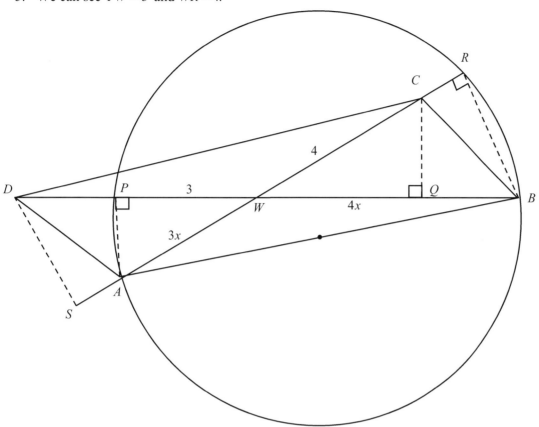

Since $\angle P$ and $\angle R$ are right angles, we know $\overline{AB}$ is the diameter of the circle.

And we can see that $\triangle APW \sim \triangle BRW$. So, $\dfrac{PW}{RW} = \dfrac{3}{4} = \dfrac{AW}{BW}$.

Let $AW = 3x$ and $BW = 4x$. $PA = \sqrt{(3x)^2 - 3^2} = 3\sqrt{x^2 - 1} \rightarrow$ Height of the parallelogram

The base of the parallelogram is $DB = 8x$. Now the area of the parallelogram in terms of x is

$8x\left(3\sqrt{x^2 - 1}\right) = 15 \rightarrow 8x\sqrt{x^2 - 1} = 5 \rightarrow 64x^2\left(x^2 - 1\right) = 25$. Let $x^2 = k$, then $d^2 = 64x^2 = 64k$

Now solve $64k(k-1) = 25 \rightarrow 64k^2 - 64k - 25 = 0 \rightarrow k = \dfrac{64 \pm \sqrt{64^2 - 4(64)(-25)}}{128} = \dfrac{64 \pm 8\sqrt{64 + 100}}{128}$

$= \dfrac{64 \pm 16\sqrt{41}}{128}$

Therefore, $d^2 = 64k = 64\left(\dfrac{64 \pm 16\sqrt{41}}{128}\right) = 32 \pm 8\sqrt{41} \rightarrow 32 + 8\sqrt{41}$ (d^2 cannot be negative)

The answer is $32 + 8 + 41 = 81$. The answer is (A).

6. Isosceles $\triangle ABC$ with $AB = AC$ and a circle are tangent at points B and C as follow.

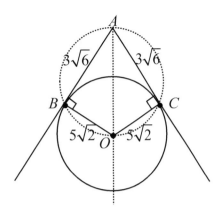

The circle passing vertices A, B, and C must pass point O, center of the circle with the radius $5\sqrt{2}$ Because quadrilateral $ABCD$ is cyclic. AO is the diameter of the dotted circle.

$$AO = \sqrt{\left(3\sqrt{6}\right)^2 + \left(5\sqrt{2}\right)^2} = 2\sqrt{26} \quad \rightarrow \quad \text{Radius} = \sqrt{26}$$

Therefore, the area of the dotted circle $= \pi\left(\sqrt{26}\right)^2 = 26\pi$.   The answer is (C).

7	Stewart's Theorem

1.

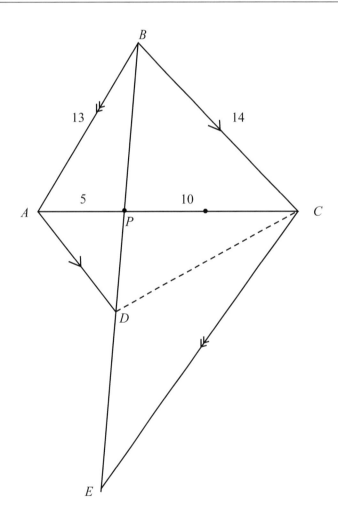

From Stewart's Theorem, $13^2(10)+14^2(5)=\left(BP^2+5\cdot10\right)(5+10)$ $\overset{\div 3}{\to}$ $169(2)+196(1)=\left(BP^2+50\right)(3)$

$338+196=\left(BP^2+50\right)\cdot3$ $\to$ $178=BP^2+50$ $\to$ $BP^2=128$ $\to$ $BP=8\sqrt{2}$

Since $\triangle ADP \sim \triangle CBP$, $PD=8\sqrt{2}\left(\dfrac{1}{2}\right)=4\sqrt{2}$. And $\triangle ABP \sim \triangle CEP$ $\to$ $PE=2\left(8\sqrt{2}\right)=16\sqrt{2}$

Therefore, $DE=16\sqrt{2}-4\sqrt{2}=12\sqrt{2}$. The answer is (D).

2.

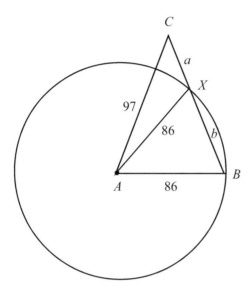

By Stewart's Theorem, $97^2(b)+86^2(a)=\left(86^2+ab\right)(a+b)$, and a and b are integers.

$97^2 b+86^2 a = 86^2 a +86^2 b+ab(a+b)$ $\to$ $\left(97^2-86^2\right)b=ab(a+b)$ $\to$ $97^2-86^2=a(a+b)$

$(97+86)(97-86)=183\cdot11=(3)(61)(11)$ $\to$ $(3)(61)(11)=a(a+b)$

By the triangular inequality, $97\sim86<a+b<97+86$ $\to$ $11<a+b<183$.

The only integer of $(a+b)$ is 61. The answer is (D).

3. For the given $BC=AM(\text{median})$, let $BM=MC=x$ and $AM=2x.$

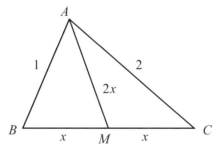

We know we should apply Stewart's theorem.

$1^2(x)+2^2(x)=\left((2x)^2+x^2\right)(x+x)$ $\to$ $5x=10x^3$ $\to$ $1=2x^2$ $\to$ $x^2=\dfrac{1}{2}$ $\to$ $x=\dfrac{\sqrt{2}}{2}$

Therefore, $BC=2\left(\dfrac{\sqrt{2}}{2}\right)=\sqrt{2}$. The answer is (C).

1.

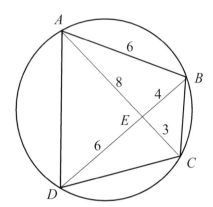

Since $8 \times 3 = 4 \times 6$, the quadrilateral is cyclic. $\triangle AEB \sim CDE$ with the ratio of 4:3.

$\dfrac{6}{DC} = \dfrac{4}{3} \rightarrow DC = 4.5$. From $\triangle BEC \sim \triangle AED$, if $BC = a$, then $AD = 2a$.

Now apply Ptolemy's Theorem.

$$(6)(4.5) + (a)(2a) = (8+3)(4+6) \rightarrow 27 + 2a^2 = 110 \rightarrow a = \sqrt{\dfrac{83}{2}}$$

Therefore, $AD = 2a = 2\sqrt{\dfrac{83}{2}} = \sqrt{166}$. The answer is (B).

2.

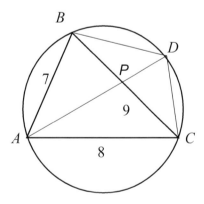

By angle bisector theorem, $\angle BAD = \angle CAD \rightarrow \overarc{BD} \cong \overarc{DC} \rightarrow BD = DC = a$
(Congruent inscribed angles have the same length of chords.)

By Ptolemy's Theorem, $8a + 7a = 9(AD) \rightarrow AD = \dfrac{15a}{9} = \dfrac{5a}{3}$

Therefore, $\dfrac{AD}{DC} = \dfrac{5a/3}{a} = \dfrac{5}{3}$. The answer is (B).

3. Let $AB = BC = CA = a$

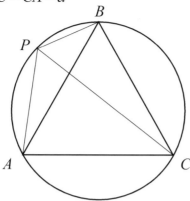

$$PB \cdot AC + PA \cdot BC = PC \cdot AB \ \rightarrow \ PB + PA = PC \quad \text{The answer is (B)}.$$

4. First, we need to recognize $AE = FD = DB = z$, $AC = BF = x$, and $AD = BE = y$.

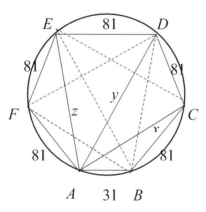

Now apply Ptolemy's Theorem.

From $\square ABCD \rightarrow 81y + 81(31) = xz \cdots\cdots(1)$ From $\square ACDF \rightarrow xz + 81(81) = y^2 \cdots\cdots(2)$

From $\square ADEF \rightarrow 81y + 81(81) = z^2 \cdots\cdots(3)$

From (1) and (2), $\ 81y + 81(31) + 81(81) = y^2 \ \rightarrow \ y^2 - 81y - 81(112) = 0$

$$y^2 - 81y - 144(63) = 0 \ \rightarrow \ (y - 144)(y + 63) = 0 \ \rightarrow \ y = 144$$

Putting $y = 144$ into (3),

$$z^2 = 81(144) + 81(81) = 81(144 + 81) = 81(225) \ \rightarrow \ z = \sqrt{81 \cdot 225} = 9(15) = 135$$

Now, (1) $\rightarrow 81(144) + 81(31) = x(135) \ \rightarrow \ x = \dfrac{81(144 + 31)}{135} = 105$

Therefore, $x + y + z = 105 + 144 + 135 = 384$.

1.

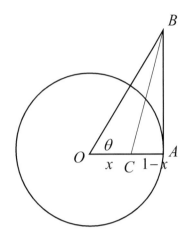

If $OC = x$, then $AC = 1 - x$.

$$\begin{cases} \cos\theta = \dfrac{1}{OB} \rightarrow OB = \dfrac{1}{\cos\theta} = \sec\theta \\[3mm] \tan\theta = \dfrac{AB}{1} \rightarrow AB = \tan\theta \end{cases}$$

By the angle bisector theorem,

$$\frac{OB}{AB} = \frac{x}{1-x} \rightarrow \frac{\sec\theta}{\tan\theta} = \frac{x}{1-x} \rightarrow x = \frac{\sec\theta}{\tan\theta + \sec\theta} = \frac{\dfrac{1}{\cos\theta}}{\dfrac{\sin\theta}{\cos\theta} + \dfrac{1}{\cos\theta}} = \frac{1}{\sin\theta + 1}$$

The answer is (D).

2. Let the radius of the third circle be r.

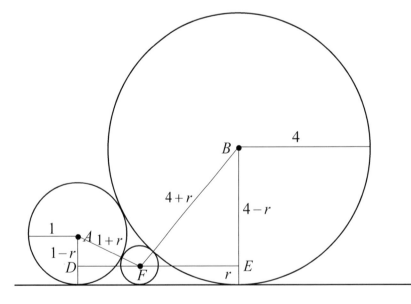

B

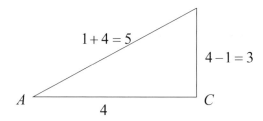

$1+4=5$

$4-1=3$

A

C

4

You can see $AC=4 \rightarrow DE=4$. And also,

$$\begin{cases} AD = 1-r \\ AF = 1+r \end{cases} \text{ and } \begin{cases} BF = 4+r \\ BE = 4-r \end{cases}$$

Since $DF+FE=4$, $\rightarrow \sqrt{(1+r)^2 - (1-r)^2} + \sqrt{(4+r)^2 - (4-r)^2} = 4$

Now solve it.

$\rightarrow \sqrt{4r} + \sqrt{16r} = 4 \rightarrow 6\sqrt{r} = 4 \rightarrow \sqrt{r} = \dfrac{2}{3} \rightarrow r = \dfrac{4}{9}$

The answer is (D).

3. Case 1) $C_1C_2 = 10-(-15) = 25$ and $DC_3 = 9-6 = 3$

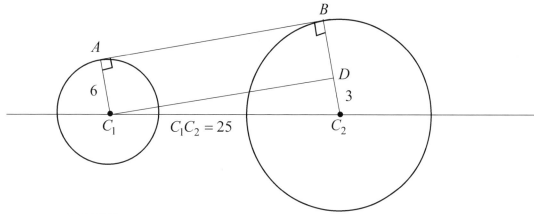

$AB = C_1D = \sqrt{25^2 - 3^2} = \sqrt{616} > 24$

Case 2)

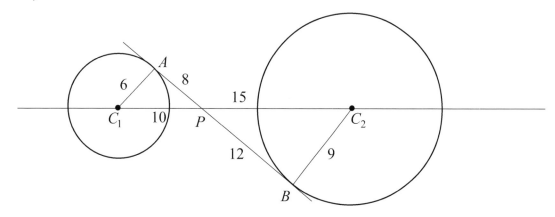

The ratio of similar triangles is 2:3. Therefore, $C_1P = 15$ and $C_2P = 10$.

By the Pythagorean theorem, $AP = 8$ and $BP = 12$. So, $AB = 8+12 = 20$.
The answer is (C).

4. The radius of the larger circle is 3. → area is 9π
    The total area of smaller circles is 7π.
    The total shaded area is $9\pi - 7\pi = 2\pi$.   The answer is (C).

5.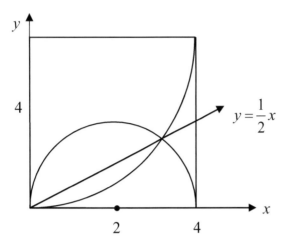

The equations of the circles are $x^2 + (y-4)^2 = 16$ and $(x-2)^2 + y^2 = 4$

$$\begin{cases} x^2 + y^2 - 8y + 16 = 16 \;\to\; x^2 + y^2 - 8y = 0 \cdots\cdots(1) \\ x^2 - 4x + 4 + y^2 = 4 \;\to\; x^2 + y^2 - 4x = 0 \cdots\cdots(2) \end{cases}$$

From $(1)-(2) \to -8y + 4x = 0 \to y = \dfrac{1}{2}x$ (This is the equation of the common chord)

Putting this in $(2) \to x^2 + \left(\dfrac{1}{2}x\right)^2 - 4x = 0 \to \dfrac{5}{4}x^2 - 4x = 0 \to \dfrac{5}{4}x\left(x - \dfrac{16}{5}\right) = 0$

We got $x = 0$ and $x = \dfrac{16}{5}$. The answer is (B).

Another approach: Using similarity

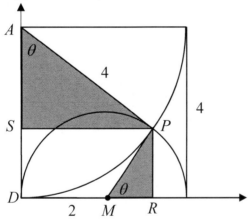

Since point P is a point of tangency, $\triangle ASP \sim \triangle MPR$.
Thus, on $\triangle MPR$, $MR = 2\cos\theta$ and $PR = 2\sin\theta$. On $\triangle ASP$, $SP = 4\sin\theta$
$SP = 2 + MR = 2 + 2\cos\theta$

Therefore, $4\sin\theta = 2 + 2\cos\theta \to 2\sin\theta = 1 + \cos\theta \to (2\sin\theta)^2 = (1+\cos\theta)^2 \to$

$$4\sin^2\theta = 1 + 2\cos\theta + \cos^2\theta \ \rightarrow \ 4\left(1 - \cos^2\theta\right) = 1 + 2\cos\theta + \cos^2\theta$$

$$\rightarrow 5\cos^2\theta + 2\cos\theta - 3 = 0 \ \rightarrow \ \left(5\cos\theta - 3\right)\left(\cos\theta + 1\right) = 0 \ \rightarrow \ \cos\theta = \frac{3}{5}, \ \left(\cos\theta \neq -1\right)$$

So, $SP = 2 + 2\cos\theta = 2 + 2\left(\dfrac{3}{5}\right) = \dfrac{16}{5}$

6. Let the radius of circle B be r.

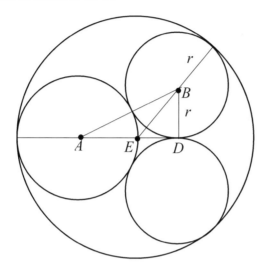

You can see $BD = r$, $BE = 2 - r$, and $AB = 1 + r$.

From $\triangle BED$, $ED = \sqrt{\left(2 - r\right)^2 - r^2} = \sqrt{4 - 4r} \ \rightarrow \ AD = 1 + \sqrt{4 - 4r}$

Now, from $\triangle ABD$, $AB^2 = BD^2 + AD^2 \ \rightarrow \ \left(1 + r\right)^2 = r^2 + \left(1 + \sqrt{4 - 4r}\right)^2 \ \rightarrow$

$1 + 2r + r^2 = r^2 + 1 + 4 - 4r + 4\sqrt{1 - r} \ \rightarrow \ 6r - 4 = 4\sqrt{1 - r} \ \rightarrow \ 3r - 2 = 2\sqrt{1 - r}$

Therefore, $\left(3r - 2\right)^2 = 4\left(1 - r\right) \ \rightarrow \ 9r^2 - 12r + 4 = 4 - 4r \ \rightarrow \ 9r^2 - 8r = 0 \rightarrow r\left(9r - 8\right) = 0$

$r \neq 0 \ \rightarrow \ 9r = 8 \ \rightarrow \ r = \dfrac{8}{9}$.   The answer is (D).

7. Let $EA = x$.

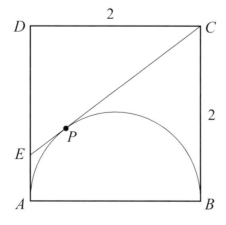

Lengths of tangents are equal. $BC = CP = 2$ and $PE = EA = x$

Therefore, $DE = 2 - x$ and $CE = 2 + x$.

By the Pythagorean theorem from $\triangle CDE$,

$$(2+x)^2 = (2-x)^2 + 2^2 \quad \rightarrow \quad 4 + 4x + x^2 = 4 - 4x + x^2 + 4 \quad \rightarrow \quad 8x = 4 \quad \rightarrow \quad x = \frac{1}{2}$$

$CE = 2 + \dfrac{1}{2} = \dfrac{5}{2}$.   The answer is (D).

8.

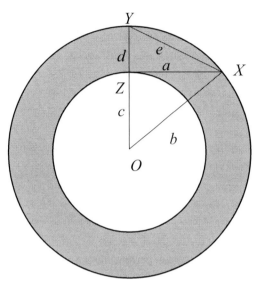

The area of the shaded region is $\pi b^2 - \pi c^2 = \pi\left(b^2 - c^2\right) = \pi a^2$.

The answer is (A).

9.

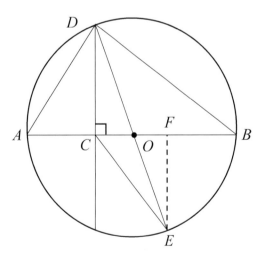

If $AC = 2$, then $BC = 4$ and $AO = 3 \rightarrow CO = 1$.

You can see that $\triangle OCD$ and $\triangle OEF$ have the same areas, because $\triangle OCD \cong \triangle OEF$ and $\triangle CEO$ and $\triangle OEF$ have the same areas.

Since $AB = 6$ and $CO = 1$,

$$\frac{\text{area of } \triangle OCD}{\text{area of } \triangle ABD} = \frac{1}{6} \ .$$

140

Therefore,

$$\frac{2\times\left(\text{area of }\Delta OCD\right)}{\text{area of }\Delta ABD}=\frac{2\times1}{6}=\frac{1}{3}.$$

The answer is (C).

10.

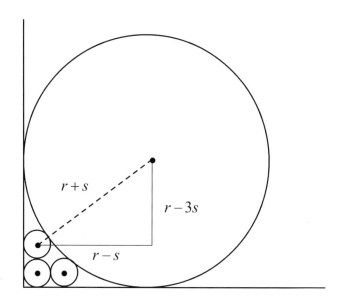

In the figure above, the length of each side $\rightarrow r+s,\ r-3s,\ r-s$

By applying the Pythagorean Theorem,

$$\left(r-3s\right)^{2}+\left(r-s\right)^{2}=\left(r+s\right)^{2}\ \rightarrow\ r^{2}-10sr+9s^{2}=0\ \rightarrow\ \left(r-9s\right)\left(r-s\right)=0$$

$r\neq s\ \rightarrow\ r=10s\ \rightarrow\ \dfrac{r}{s}=9$ The answer is (D). You also cause use $s=1$.

11.

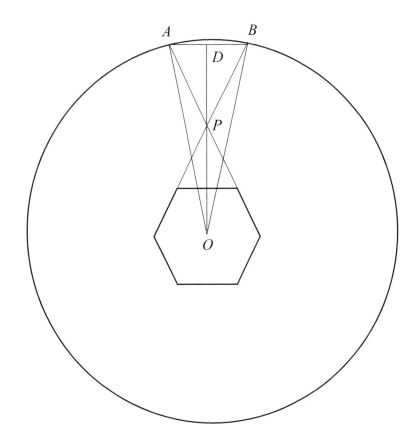

To have the probability of $\dfrac{1}{2}$, the total measure of arc is $\dfrac{360°}{2} = 180°$. Each measure of arc is

$\dfrac{180°}{6} = 30°. \ \rightarrow \ \angle AOB = 30°.$ We can see $OP = 2\left(\sqrt{3}\right) = 2\sqrt{3}$.

Since $\triangle APO$ isosceles, $AP = PO = 2\sqrt{3}$. ($\angle POA = 15°$, $\angle APO = 150°$ $\rightarrow$ $\angle PAO = 15°$)

$\triangle ABP$ is equilateral and $AB = AP = 2\sqrt{3}$ and $BD = \dfrac{2\sqrt{3}}{2} = \sqrt{3}$.

Now $\sin \angle BOD = \dfrac{DB}{OB} \ \rightarrow \ \sin 15° = \dfrac{\sqrt{3}}{r}$.

Remember.

$\sin 15 = \sin\left(45 - 30\right) = \sin 45 \cos 30 - \cos 45 \sin 30 = \dfrac{\sqrt{2}}{2}\left(\dfrac{\sqrt{3}}{2}\right) - \dfrac{\sqrt{2}}{2}\left(\dfrac{1}{2}\right) = \dfrac{\sqrt{6} - \sqrt{2}}{4}$

So, $\dfrac{\sqrt{6} - \sqrt{2}}{4} = \dfrac{\sqrt{3}}{r} \ \rightarrow \ r = \left(\dfrac{4\sqrt{3}}{\sqrt{6} - \sqrt{2}}\right)\left(\dfrac{\sqrt{6} + \sqrt{2}}{\sqrt{6} + \sqrt{2}}\right) = \dfrac{\cancel{4}\sqrt{3}\left(\sqrt{6} + \sqrt{2}\right)}{\cancel{4}} = 3\sqrt{2} + \sqrt{6}$.

The answer is (D).

Or, simply

$DP = 3$ and $OD = 3 + 2\sqrt{3}$. By Pythagorean theorem,

$r = \sqrt{\left(\sqrt{3}\right)^2 + \left(3 + 2\sqrt{3}\right)^2} = \sqrt{24 + 2\sqrt{108}} = \sqrt{18 + 6 + 2\sqrt{108}} = \sqrt{18} + \sqrt{6} = 3\sqrt{2} + \sqrt{6}$

12.

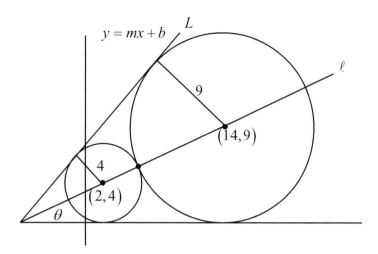

We can see $\tan\theta = \dfrac{9-4}{14-2} = \dfrac{5}{12}$ (Slope of line ℓ)

$m = \tan(2\theta) = \dfrac{2\tan\theta}{1-\tan^2\theta}$ (Slope of line L),

$m = \tan(2\theta) = \dfrac{2\tan\theta}{1-\tan^2\theta} = \dfrac{2\left(\dfrac{5}{12}\right)}{1-\left(\dfrac{5}{12}\right)^2} = \dfrac{120}{119}$

Equation of line ℓ: $y = \dfrac{5}{12}x + b$ passing through point $(2,4)$

$4 = \dfrac{5}{12}(2)+b \rightarrow b = 4 - \dfrac{5}{6} = \dfrac{19}{6}$. Therefore, the equation of line ℓ: $y = \dfrac{5}{12}x + \dfrac{19}{6}$

Now find x-intercept. $0 = \dfrac{5}{12}x + \dfrac{19}{6} \rightarrow x = -\dfrac{38}{5} \rightarrow \left(-\dfrac{38}{5}, 0\right)$

Line L with $y = \dfrac{120}{119}x + b$ passes through point $\left(-\dfrac{38}{5}, 0\right)$.

Therefore, $0 = \dfrac{120}{119}\left(-\dfrac{38}{5}\right)+b \rightarrow b = \dfrac{120}{119}\left(\dfrac{38}{5}\right) = \dfrac{912}{119}$. The answer is (E).

13.

   case 1)

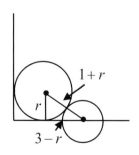

Using Pythagorean Theorem,

$(1+r)^2 = r^2 + (3-r)^2 \rightarrow 1+2r+r^2 = r^2 + 9 - 6r + r^2$

$r^2 - 8r + 8 = 0$

Case 2)

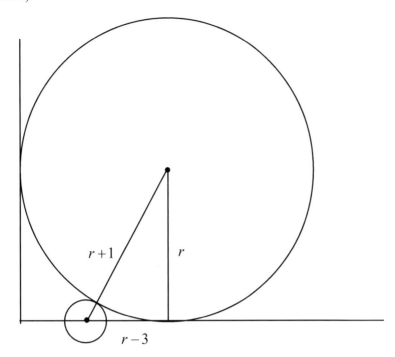

Pythagorean Theorem: $(1+r)^2 = r^2 + (r-3)^2$ yields the exact same equation.

Therefore, sum of the roots of $r^2 - 8r + 8 = 0$ is $-\dfrac{b}{a} = -\dfrac{-8}{1} = 8$.   The answer is (D).

14. We have two different cases.

Case 1) $k > 0$

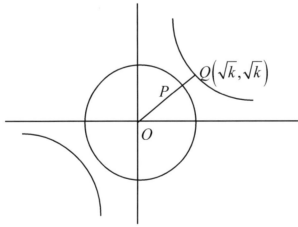

We can see that $OP = k$ and $OQ = \sqrt{2}\sqrt{k}$.

In order not to have intersection,

$$OQ > OP \;\rightarrow\; \sqrt{2k} > k \;\rightarrow\; 2k > k^2 \;\rightarrow\; k^2 - 2k < 0 \;\rightarrow\; k(k-2) < 0$$

Therefore, $0 < k < 2$ $\rightarrow k = 1$ (Integer)

Case 2) $k < 0$

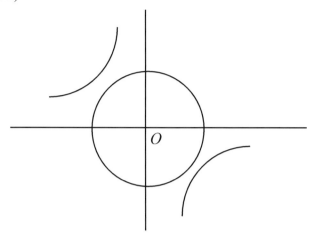

Same as case 1, $\quad 0 < -k < 2 \;\rightarrow\; -2 < k < 0 \;\rightarrow\; k = -1.$

Therefore, there are two integers 1 and -1. The answer is (C).

15.

$$DE: \quad \frac{3}{4} = \frac{8}{DE} \;\rightarrow\; DE = \frac{32}{4} = 8$$

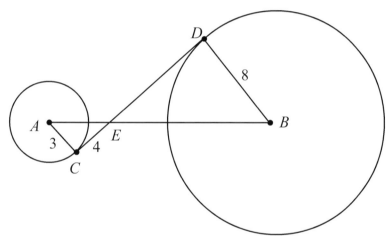

Therefore, $CD = 4 + \dfrac{32}{3} = \dfrac{44}{3}$. The answer is (B).

16. $(x+y)^2 = x^2 + y^2 \;\rightarrow\; 2xy = 0$

Solutions: $x = 0$ or $y = 0 \;\rightarrow\;$ Two perpendicular lines. The answer is (C).

17.

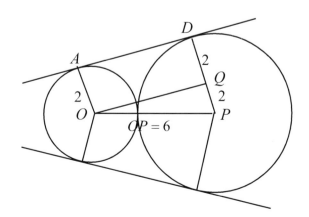

$OQ = \sqrt{6^2 - 2^2} = 4\sqrt{2}$ and area of $OADP$ is $\left(2 \cdot 4\sqrt{2}\right) + \left(\dfrac{2 \cdot 4\sqrt{2}}{2}\right) = 12\sqrt{2}$.

Therefore, the area of $AOBCPD$ is $2\left(12\sqrt{2}\right) = 24\sqrt{2}$. The answer is (B).

18.

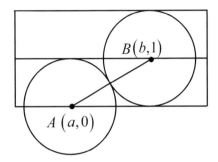

As we can see in the figure above, if $AB \leq 2$, then the circles are intersected.

$$\sqrt{(a-b)^2 + (1-0)^2} \leq 2 \rightarrow (a-b)^2 \leq 3 \rightarrow |a-b| \leq \sqrt{3}$$

Now we got

$$-\sqrt{3} \leq a - b \leq \sqrt{3} \rightarrow \begin{cases} b \leq a + \sqrt{3} \\ b \geq a - \sqrt{3} \end{cases} \quad \text{and } 0 \leq a \leq 2 \text{ and } 0 \leq b \leq 2$$

Now graph

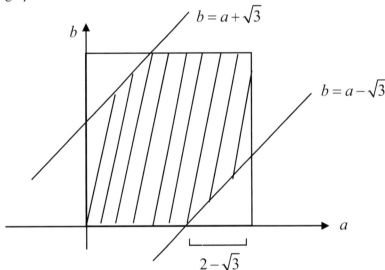

Sum of areas of the triangles is $2\left(\dfrac{\left(2 - \sqrt{3}\right)\left(2 - \sqrt{3}\right)}{2}\right) = 7 - 4\sqrt{3}$.

The area of the shaded region is $4 - \left(7 - 4\sqrt{3}\right) = 4\sqrt{3} - 3$

Therefore, the geometric probability is

$$P = \frac{4\sqrt{3} - 3}{4}.$$

The answer is (E).

19.

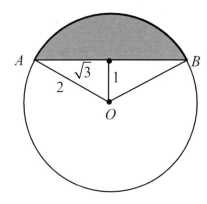

$\angle AOB = 120°$ and the area of the shaded region is $\dfrac{4\pi}{3} - \sqrt{3}.$

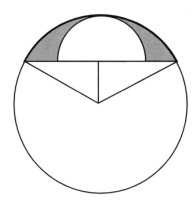

Now subtract the area of the semi-circle from the area of shaded region.

$$\frac{4\pi}{3} - \sqrt{3} - \frac{\pi}{2} = \frac{5\pi}{6} - \sqrt{3}$$

Therefore, the total area of the shaded region is

$$2\left(\frac{5\pi}{6} - \sqrt{3}\right) = \frac{5\pi}{3} - 2\sqrt{3}. \text{ The answer is (B).}$$

1. Using their centers,

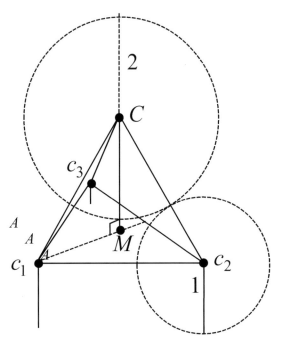

We can see that the length of $\overline{c_1 M}$ $\left(\dfrac{2}{3}$ of the median$\right)$ is $\dfrac{2}{3}\times\sqrt{3}=\dfrac{2\sqrt{3}}{3}$ and

$$c_1 C = 1+2 = 3.$$

Now, $CM = \sqrt{3^2 - \left(\dfrac{2\sqrt{3}}{3}\right)^2} = \sqrt{9-\dfrac{12}{9}} = \sqrt{\dfrac{81-12}{9}} = \dfrac{\sqrt{69}}{3}$

Therefore, the distance from bottom to the top is $1+2+\dfrac{\sqrt{69}}{3} = 3+\dfrac{\sqrt{69}}{3}$.

The answer is (B).

2. First, recognize the view from top as follows. Three spheres are tangent.

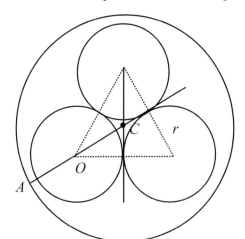

$$AC = 5$$

$$OC = r\sqrt{3}\times\dfrac{2}{3} = \dfrac{2r\sqrt{3}}{3}$$

The figure from front:

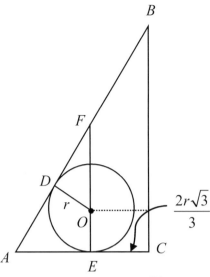

$$AC = 5 = AE + EC \quad \rightarrow \quad EC = \frac{2r\sqrt{3}}{3}$$

We can see that $\triangle ABC \sim \triangle AEF \sim \triangle DEF$, and ratio of the right triangle is 5:12:13.

So, if $OD = r,$ then $OF = \frac{13}{5}r$. $EF = \frac{13}{5}r + r = \frac{18}{5}r$

From $\triangle ABC \sim \triangle AEF$, $AE = EF \times \frac{5}{12} = \frac{18}{5}r \times \frac{5}{12} = \frac{3}{2}r$

Now, $AC = AE + EC \quad \rightarrow \quad 5 = \frac{3r}{2} + \frac{2r\sqrt{3}}{3}$, multiply by 6

$30 = 9r + 4r\sqrt{3} \rightarrow 30 = r\left(9 + 4\sqrt{3}\right) \rightarrow r = \frac{30}{9 + 4\sqrt{3}}$

Therefore, $r = \frac{30\left(9 - 4\sqrt{3}\right)}{\left(9 + 4\sqrt{3}\right)\left(9 - 4\sqrt{3}\right)} = \frac{30\left(9 - 4\sqrt{3}\right)}{33} = \frac{90 - 40\sqrt{3}}{11}$. The answer is (D).

| 11 | Similar Figures |

1.

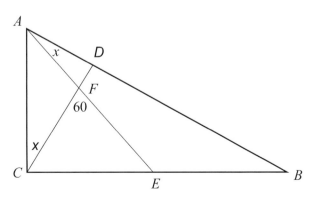

Given: $AB = 2 \cdot AC$, $\angle BAE = \angle ACD = a$, and $\triangle CEF$ is equilateral $\rightarrow \angle AFD = 60$

You can see that $\triangle AFD \sim \triangle ACD$ by $AA \cong AA$, $\angle ADF = \angle CDA$(Common).
Therefore, the corresponding angles $\angle CAD = \angle AFD = 60$. Since $AB = 2 \cdot AC$ and
$\angle CAD = 60$, the triangle must be a right triangle. $\angle ACB$ must be right angle. The answer is (C).

2.

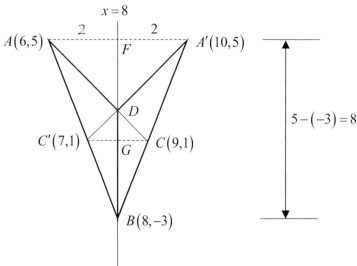

The area of the union of the two triangles = area of $\triangle AA'B$ – area of $\triangle AA'B$

$[\triangle AA'B] = \dfrac{4 \times 8}{2} = 16$ and $FG = 4$. Since $\triangle AA'D \sim \triangle CC'D$, the factor of similitude is 2:1 and

$FG = 5$. So, $FD = 4 \times \dfrac{2}{3} = \dfrac{8}{3}$

Therefore, $[\triangle AA'D] = \dfrac{1}{2}\left(4 \times \dfrac{8}{3}\right) = \dfrac{16}{3}$ and the area of the union is $16 - \dfrac{16}{3} = \dfrac{32}{3}$.

The answer is (E).

3. The easiest way to find $DF = DE - FE$

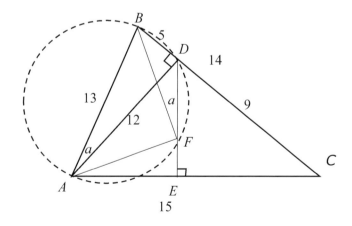

Step1) Find AD. Using Heron's formula

Area of $\triangle ABC = \sqrt{s(s-a)(s-b)(s-c)}$ and $s = \dfrac{a+b+c}{2} = \dfrac{13+14+15}{2} = 21$

$$\text{Area} = \sqrt{21(21-13)(21-14)(21-15)} = \sqrt{21 \cdot 8 \cdot 7 \cdot 6} = 84$$

$$\frac{14 \cdot AD}{2} = 84 \rightarrow AD = 12, \ BD = 5, \text{ and } DE = \frac{AD \cdot DC}{AC} = \frac{12 \cdot 9}{15} = \frac{36}{5}$$

$$12^2 = AE \cdot 15 \rightarrow AE = \frac{144}{15} = \frac{48}{5}$$

Step 2) $\triangle ABD \sim \triangle AFE \ (AA \cong AA)$, because $\angle BAD = \angle BFD = a$ (cyclic)

Therefore, $\angle ABD = \angle AFE = 90 - a$. Now you can see $\triangle ABD \sim \triangle AFE$.

$$\frac{FE}{AE} = \frac{5}{12} \rightarrow \frac{FE}{48/5} = \frac{5}{12} \rightarrow FE = \frac{48}{12} = 4$$

Therefore, $DF = \frac{36}{5} - 4 = \frac{16}{5} \rightarrow 16 + 5 = 21$. The answer is (B).

4.

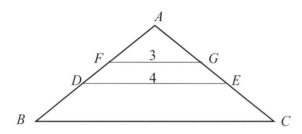

Since the ratio of FG to $DE = 3 : 4$, the ratio of areas of $\triangle AFG$ to $\triangle ADE$ is $3^2 : 4^2$.

If the area of $\triangle ADE$ is $9k$ and the area of $\triangle ADE$ is $16k$, $[\triangle DEGF] = 16k - 9k = 7k = 7$.

(Note: $[\triangle DEFG]$ means the area of the figure.)

Now, $[\triangle ADE] = 16k = 16(1) = 16$. Therefore, $[\square DBCA] = 40 - 16 = 24$. The answer is (D).

5. The resulting figure is as follows. DE is the crease and $AD = DB = 2.5$.

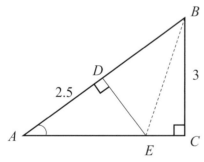

You can see that $\triangle ADE \sim \triangle ACB$ by $aa \cong aa$.

Therefore, $\frac{2.5}{DE} = \frac{4}{3} \rightarrow DE = \frac{7.5}{4} = \frac{15}{8}$. The answer is (D).

6.

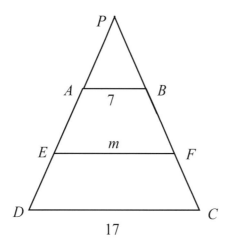

Since $\Delta PAB \sim \Delta PEF \sim \Delta PDC$, ratio of their corresponding sides is $7:n:17$.
The ratio of their areas is $7^2:m^2:17^2 = 49:m^2:289$.
To have the same area,
$$m^2 - 49 = 289 - m^2 \rightarrow 2m^2 = 289 + 49 \rightarrow 2m^2 = 339 \rightarrow m^2 = 169$$
Therefore, $m = 13$. The answer is (D).

7.

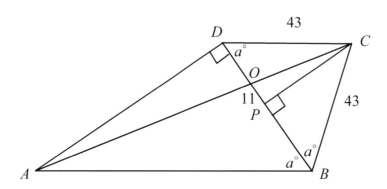

$\angle CDP = \angle CBP$ (Isosceles triangle) and equal to $\angle DBA$ (Alternate interior angle)
Since $\Delta ADB \sim \Delta CBP$, $\dfrac{AB}{43} = \dfrac{2}{1} \rightarrow AB = 86$.

Ans also, $\Delta CDO \sim \Delta ABO$. Let $PB = x$. $\dfrac{DO}{BO} = \dfrac{43}{86} \rightarrow \dfrac{x-11}{x+11} = \dfrac{1}{2} \rightarrow x = 33$

Now $BD = 66$, and by Pythagorean theorem,
$$AD^2 = 86^2 - 66^2 = (86+66)(86-66) = 152 \cdot 20 \rightarrow AD = \sqrt{4 \cdot 38 \cdot 4 \cdot 5} = 4\sqrt{190}$$
Therefore, $m + 4 = 194$. The answer is (D).

This represents the point divided in the ratio of $3^{96}:2^{96}$ as follows.

$$\underset{A(16)}{\bullet}\xrightarrow{\hspace{2cm}3^{96}\hspace{1.5cm}:\hspace{1cm}2^{96}\hspace{1cm}}\underset{P}{\bullet}\quad\underset{B(81)}{\bullet}$$

You can see the number P must be a little less than 81.

$\overline{AB} = 81 - 16 = 65$ and $\dfrac{AP}{PB} = \dfrac{3^{96}}{2^{96}} = \left(\dfrac{3}{2}\right)^{96} \approx 8 \times 10^{16}$ Extremely large number.

Therefore, $p \approx 16 + 65\left(\dfrac{8 \times 10^6}{8 \times 10^6 + 1}\right) \approx 81$ (but less than 81).

So, the greatest integer must be 80. The answer is (A).

2. The coordinates are as follows.

$$\left(\frac{1(9) + 2(-9)}{1+2}, \frac{1(-4) + 2(8)}{1+2}\right) = \left(\frac{-9}{3}, \frac{12}{3}\right) = (-3, 4) \qquad \text{The answer is (B)}.$$

3.

$$\frac{2^{302} + 3^{302}}{2^{300} + 3^{300}} = \frac{4\left(2^{300}\right) + 9\left(3^{300}\right)}{2^{300} + 3^{300}}$$

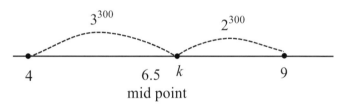

4 \qquad 6.5 k \qquad 9
mid point

Since $3^{300} > 2^{300}$, the value of k lie right after 6.5 but less than 9.
The answer is (D).

1. $EF = \dfrac{1(17) + 1(7)}{2} = 12$. The answer is (D).

2. $EF = \dfrac{2(10) + 5(6)}{2+5} = \dfrac{50}{7}$. The answer is (B).

3. $\dfrac{AE}{ED} = \dfrac{BF}{FC} = \dfrac{3}{2}$ $\rightarrow$ $BF = 15 \times \dfrac{3}{5} = 9$ and $EF = \dfrac{3(12) + 2(6)}{5} = 9.6$

Therefore, the area of $ABEF = \dfrac{(9.6 + 6)9}{2} = 70.2$. The answer is (D).

1. $A(h) =$ the height of a pillar.

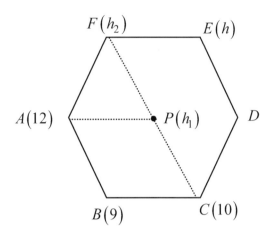

By the theorem, since $AB = CP$ and $\overline{A(12)B(9)} \parallel \overline{C(10)P(h_1)}$, $h_1 = 10 + (12 - 9) = 13$.

At point F, $h_2 = 13 + 3 = 16 \rightarrow F(16)$

Now, $EF = BC$ and $\overline{F(16)E(h)} \parallel \overline{B(9)C(10)}$.

Therefore, $h = 16 + (10 - 9) = 17$. The answer is (D).

15 | Trace by a disk around a square

1. Case 1: Trace outside of a square

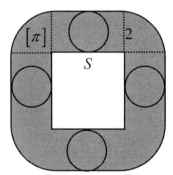

Area of the region: $A = 4(2s) + 4\pi = 8s + 4\pi$

Case 2: Trace inside of a square

area of a square $= 1 \times 1 = 1$ (12 squares)

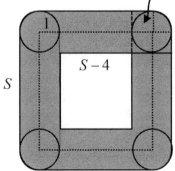

Area of the region: $B = 4\left[2(s-4)\right] + 12(1) + 4\left(\dfrac{\pi}{4}\right) = 8s - 20 + \pi$

Since $A = 2B$,

$8s + 4\pi = 2(8s - 20 + \pi) \rightarrow 8s = 2\pi + 40$

$s = 5 + \dfrac{\pi}{4} \rightarrow a = 5, b = 1, c = 4 \rightarrow a + b + c = 10$. Answer is (A).

1. From the figure, the perimeter of $\triangle BEC = 12 + 10 + 10 = 32$ and

   the perimeter of $\triangle AED = \sqrt{(x+6)^2} + \sqrt{(x+6)^2} + 2x + 12$.

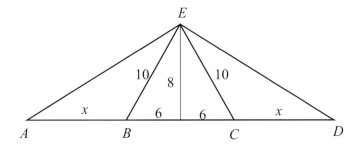

   Now set up the equation.

   $2\sqrt{(x+6)^2} + 2x + 12 = 2(32)$ → $\sqrt{(x+6)^2} = 26 - x$ → $x^2 + 12x + 36 = 676 - 52x + x^2$ →

   $64x = 576$ → $x = 9$. Answer is (D).

2. From the figure, the area of $ABCD = \dfrac{(39+52)h}{2}$ and $h^2 = 5^2 - a^2 = 12^2 - (13-a)^2$.

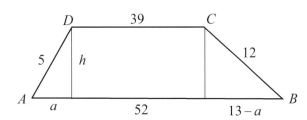

   $5^2 - a^2 = 12^2 - (13-a)^2$ → $25 - a^2 = 144 - 169 + 26a - a^2$ → $a = \dfrac{25}{13}$

   Now $h^2 = 25 - \left(\dfrac{25}{13}\right)^2$ → $h = \sqrt{\dfrac{25 \cdot 13^2 - 25^2}{13^2}} = \dfrac{\sqrt{25(13^2 - 25)}}{13} = \dfrac{\sqrt{25 \cdot 144}}{13} = \dfrac{5 \cdot 12}{13}$

   Therefore, the area is $= \dfrac{(39+52)}{2} \cdot \dfrac{5 \cdot 12}{13} = \dfrac{91}{2} \cdot \dfrac{60}{13} = 210$. Answer is (C).

   Or, just simply, draw line $\overline{DE}$ parallel to line $\overline{BC}$.

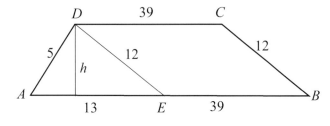

   We can see $\{5,12,13\}$ are right triangle triplet. Triangle ADE is a right triangle. So, area of triangle

ADE is $\dfrac{5\times 12}{2}=\dfrac{13\times h}{2}\;\rightarrow\;h=\dfrac{60}{13}$. Therefore, the area is $=\dfrac{(39+52)}{2}\cdot\dfrac{60}{13}=\dfrac{91}{2}\cdot\dfrac{60}{13}=210$.

3. From the figure, triangles at corner are isosceles. Now we got $GD=2+2\sqrt{2}$ and $RG=h=2+\sqrt{2}$.

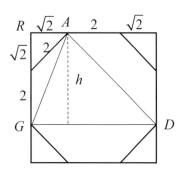

Therefore, the area of $\triangle ADG$ is $\dfrac{\left(2+2\sqrt{2}\right)\left(2+\sqrt{2}\right)}{2}=4+3\sqrt{2}$. Answer is (C).

4.

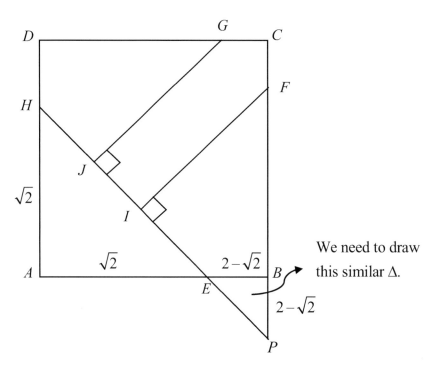

We can see the area of the square is 4. $\rightarrow$ $AB=2$.

Since the area of $\triangle AHE$ is 1, $HA=AE=\sqrt{2}$ and $EB=BP=2-\sqrt{2}$

Area of $\triangle EBP=\dfrac{\left(2-\sqrt{2}\right)\left(2-\sqrt{2}\right)}{2}=3-2\sqrt{2}$. ($\triangle EBP$ is isosceles)

Now the area of $\triangle IFP=1+3-2\sqrt{2}=4-2\sqrt{2}$. ($\triangle IFB$ is isosceles and $FI=IP$.)

$\dfrac{FI\times IP}{2}=\dfrac{FI^{2}}{2}=4-2\sqrt{2}\;\rightarrow\;FI^{2}=8-4\sqrt{2}$

The answer is (B).

156

5.

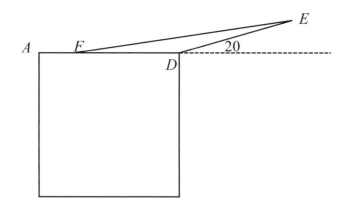

Since $FD = DE$, $\angle F + \angle E = 20$ and $\angle F = 10$. Therefore, $\measuredangle AFE = 180 - 10 = 170$.

| 17 | Graphs of $|x| + |y| = c$ and $|x| - |y| = c$ |

1. The graphs of $x + 3y = 3$ and $\left||x| - |y|\right| = 1$ are as follows. $x + 3y = 3 \rightarrow y = -\frac{1}{3}x + 1$

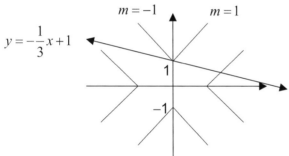

In the figure above, you can see three points of intersection. The answer is (C).

2. The maximum occurs at the corner $(4, 0)$. $Max P = 2(4) + 0 = 8$

Or $P = 2x + y \rightarrow y = -2x + P$

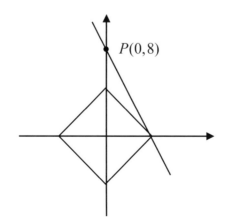

The answer is (E).

3. $x^2 + 3y = 9 \rightarrow y = -\dfrac{1}{3}x^2 + 3$

   $(|x| + |y| - 4) = 1, -1 \rightarrow |x| + |y| = 5, 3$ The graphs will be diamonds.

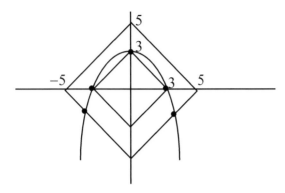

   We can see five intersections on the graphs above. The answer is (D).

| 18 | Identical Equation |

1. $8xy - 12y + 2x - 3 = 0 \rightarrow 4y(2x-3) + (2x-3) = 0 \rightarrow (2x-3)(4y+1) = 0$

   For all y, it should be 0. Therefore, $2x - 3 = 0 \rightarrow x = \dfrac{3}{2}$. The answer is (A).

2. $xy - 10x + 24y = 2x + 288 \rightarrow xy - 12x + 24y = 288 \rightarrow x(y-12) + 24(y-12) = 0$

   $(x+24)(y-12) = 0 \rightarrow x + 24 = 0$. The answer is (D).

| 19 | Average Speed (Average Rate of Change) |

1. Let the time be x. Set up the distance d using two different speeds 40mph and 60mph.

   $d = 40\left(x + \dfrac{3}{60}\right) = 60\left(x - \dfrac{3}{60}\right) \rightarrow 40x + 2 = 60x - 3 \rightarrow 20x = 5 \rightarrow x = \dfrac{1}{4}$ hours.

   Now $d = 40\left(\dfrac{1}{4} + \dfrac{3}{60}\right) = 12$ miles. Therefore, on time speed is $\dfrac{12}{1/4} = 48$ mph.

   The answer is (B).

| 20 | Relative Speed |

1. Define the speed of the boat V_s and the speed of Emily V_e.

   When Emily is walking along with the boat. Relative to an observer on the boat, her speed is $V_1 = V_e - V_s$.

   When Emily is walking in the opposite direction. Relative to an observer on the boat, her speed is $V_2 = V_e + V_s$.

158

Since Emily takes 210 steps to walk along with the boat and 42 steps to walk opposite the boat, that means it takes her 5 times longer to walk the length of a stationary boat at $V_e - V_s$ compared to $V_e + V_s$. Therefore, the ratio of the relative speeds is

$$\frac{V_2}{V_1} = \frac{V_e + V_s}{V_e - V_s} = \frac{5}{1}$$

This means that $5V_e - 5V_s = V_e + V_s \rightarrow V_s = \frac{2}{3}V_e$. Thus $V_1 = V_e - V_s = V_e - \frac{2}{3}V_e = \frac{1}{3}V_e$.

As Emily takes 210 steps to walk the length of the boat at a speed of V_1, she must take $\frac{1}{3}$ of the time to walk the length of the boat at a speed of V_e. so, the answer is $210 \times \frac{1}{3} = 70$.

The answer is (A).

21	Algebra with Integers (Special equation)

1. $a^2 - b^2 = 9 \rightarrow (a+b)(a-b) = 9$. Since $a > b$, $a + b = 9$ and $a - b = 1$. When you solve the system of equations, $a = 5$ and $b = 4$.

2. $\frac{1}{a} + \frac{1}{b} = \frac{1}{13} \rightarrow \frac{a+b}{ab} = \frac{1}{13} \rightarrow ab - 13a - 13b = 0$. Now make a product form as follows.

   $a(b-13) - 13(b-13) = 169 \rightarrow (a-13)(b-13) = 169$. Since $a > b$, $a - 13 = 169$ and $b - 13 = 1$.

   Therefore, $a = 182$ and $b = 14$.

3. By multiplying its common denominator xy: $x + \frac{2}{x} = y + \frac{2}{y} \rightarrow x^2 y + 2y = xy^2 + 2x$

   Factor: $x^2 y - xy^2 - 2x + 2y = 0 \rightarrow xy(x-y) - 2(x-y) = 0 \rightarrow (x-y)(xy-2) = 0$

   Since $x \neq y$, we got $xy - 2 = 0 \rightarrow xy = 2$. The answer is (D).

4. Completing square: $x^2 + y^2 = 10x - 6y - 34 \rightarrow x^2 - 10x + y^2 + 6y = -34 \rightarrow$

   $(x-5)^2 + (y+3)^2 = 0$ represents a point $x = 5$ and $y = -3$. (Not a circle)

   Therefore, $x + y = 2$. The answer is (B).

5. First we check the valve of k so that the equation has real solutions. (Discriminant ≥ 0)

   $D = k^2 - 4(5)(12) \geq 0 \rightarrow k^2 \geq 240 \rightarrow k \geq \sqrt{240}$ or $k \leq -\sqrt{240}$

   Since $-200 < k < 200$, we got that $-200 < k < -\sqrt{240}$ and $\sqrt{240} \leq k < 200$.

   Now using sum and product of the roots, a and b We assume a is an integer.

   Sum: $a + b = -\frac{k}{5}$ and product $ab = \frac{12}{5} \rightarrow b = \frac{12}{5a}$

   Now $a + b = -\frac{k}{5} \rightarrow k = -(5a + 5b) \rightarrow -k = -\left(5a + 5\left(\frac{12}{5a}\right)\right) \rightarrow k = -\left(5a + \frac{12}{a}\right)$

   a. For the interval $-200 < k \leq -\sqrt{240}$,

   $-200 < -\left(5a + \frac{12}{a}\right) \leq -\sqrt{240} \rightarrow \sqrt{240} \leq 5a + \frac{12}{a} < 200$

159

We can see that inequality $\sqrt{240} \le 5a + \dfrac{12}{a} < 200$ is true for $a = 1, 2, 3, 4, \cdots 39$.

Since there are 39 numbers of a, there must be 39 numbers of k.

b. For the interval $\sqrt{240} \le k < 200$, the inequality is $-200 \le 5a + \dfrac{12}{a} < -\sqrt{250}$.

We also can see that inequality $-200 < 5a + \dfrac{12}{a} \le -\sqrt{240}$ is true for $a = -1, -2, -3, -4, \cdots, -39$.

Therefore, there are $2 \times 39 = 78$ numbers k. The answer is (E).

6. To have integer values of $\dfrac{n}{30-n}$, $\dfrac{n}{30-n} \ge 1$ $\rightarrow$ $n \ge 30 - n$ $\rightarrow$ $n \ge 15$. We can see, when

$n = 15$, $\dfrac{15}{30-15} = 1$ giving integer. Also we can see denomerater $30 - n$ must be positive.

$30 - n > 0$ $\rightarrow$ $n < 30$. Now we check $\dfrac{15}{15}, \dfrac{16}{14}, \dfrac{17}{13}, \cdots, \dfrac{20}{10}, \cdots, \dfrac{24}{6}, \cdots, \dfrac{25}{5}, \cdots, \dfrac{27}{3}, \cdots, \dfrac{28}{2}, \dfrac{29}{1}$.

There are seven integers n such as $15, 20, 24, 25, 27, 28,$ and 29.

Or, let $\dfrac{n}{30-n} = k$, where $k = $ integer. Then $\dfrac{n}{30-n} = k$ $\rightarrow$ $n = \dfrac{30k}{k+1}$.

We can see k and $k+1$ are relatively prime. To have integer n, $k+1$ should divide

30. Therefore, $k+1 = 1, 2, 3, 5, 6, 10, 15, 30$ $\rightarrow$ $k = \cancel{0}, 1, 2, 4, 5, 9, 14, 29$ (k cannot be 0)
The answer is (D).

7. $x + y + xy = 80$ $\rightarrow$ $x(y+1) + (y+1) = 80 + 1$ $\rightarrow$ $(x+1)(y+1) = 81$

We can see that $x + 1 = 27$ and $y + 1 = 3$. Therefore $x = 26$.
The answer is (E).

8. $4000 \cdot \left(\dfrac{2}{5}\right)^n = 2^5 \cdot 5^3 \cdot \left(\dfrac{2^n}{5^n}\right)$

1) If $n \ge 0$, then $n = 0, 1, 2, 3$. 2) If $n < 0$, $2^5 \cdot 5^3 \cdot \left(\dfrac{5^{-n}}{2^{-n}}\right)$, then $n = -1, -2, -3, -4, -5$.

Therefore, total number is 9. The answer is (E).

9. You can see one equation with two variables. Let's modify the equation.

$\sqrt{\log a} + \sqrt{\log b} + \dfrac{\log a}{2} + \dfrac{\log b}{2} = 100$ $\rightarrow$ $\log a + 2\sqrt{\log a} + \log b + 2\sqrt{\log b} = 200$ $\rightarrow$

$\left(\log a + 2\sqrt{\log a} + 1\right) + \left(\log b + 2\sqrt{\log b} + 1\right) = 202$ $\rightarrow$ $\left(\sqrt{\log a} + 1\right)^2 + \left(\sqrt{\log b} + 1\right)^2 = 202$

From the equation, you need to find two squares whose sum is 202 such that

$9^2 + 11^2 = 202$, because $\sqrt{\log a} + 1$ and $\sqrt{\log b} + 1$ are integers.

Therefore, $\sqrt{\log a} + 1 = 9$ $\rightarrow$ $\log a = 64$ and $\sqrt{\log b} + 1 = 11$ $\rightarrow$ $\log b = 100$

Now $a = 10^{64}$ and $b = 10^{100}$ $\rightarrow$ $ab = 10^{64} \cdot 10^{100} = 10^{164}$. The answer is (D).

10. $x^{2020} + y^2 = 2y \rightarrow x^{2020} + y^2 - 2y + 1 = 1 \leftrightarrow x^{2020} + (y-1)^2 = 1$

Case 1: $\begin{cases} x^{2020} = 1 \\ (y-1)^2 = 0 \end{cases} \rightarrow x = \pm 1, \ y = 1 \rightarrow (1,1), (-1,1)$

Case 2: $\begin{cases} x^{2020} = 0 \\ (y-1)^2 = 1 \end{cases} \rightarrow x = 0, \ y = 2, 0 \rightarrow (0,2), (0,0)$

Total of 4 ordered pairs $\rightarrow$ The answer is (D).

11. $x^2 + y^2 = 10x - 6y - 34 \rightarrow x^2 + y^2 - 10x + 6y = -34 \rightarrow (x-5)^2 + (y+3)^2 = 0$

$x + 5, \ y = -3 \rightarrow x + y = 5 + (-3) = 2$ The answer is (B).

12. Let $x = \text{lcm}(a,b), y = \gcd(a,b)$. We know $ab = xy$ and $x > y$.

Now the equation is

$xy + 63 = 20x + 12y \rightarrow xy - 20x - 12y = -63 \rightarrow x(y-20) - 12(y-20) = 240 - 63$

$(x-12)(y-20) = 177 \rightarrow$ There are two different combinations as follows.

$\begin{cases} x - 12 = 177 \\ y - 20 = 1 \end{cases}$ or $\begin{cases} x - 12 = 59 \\ y - 20 = 3 \end{cases} \rightarrow$ Solutions are $\begin{cases} x = 189 \\ y = 21 \end{cases}$ and $\begin{cases} x = 71 \\ y = 23 \end{cases}$

Remember: $\text{lcm}(a,b)$ is a multiple of $\gcd(a,b)$. The only solution is $\begin{cases} x = \text{lcm}(a,b) = 189 \\ y = \gcd(a,b) = 21 \end{cases}$.

Therefore, (a,b) must be $\begin{array}{c|cc} 21 & a & b \\ \hline & 1 & 9 \end{array}$ or $\begin{array}{c|cc} 21 & a & b \\ \hline & 9 & 1 \end{array}$. $\rightarrow (21, 189), (189, 21)$

The answer is (B).

13. Define two integer zeros: r_1 and r_2.

Sum of the roots: $r_1 + r_2 = a$ and Product of the roots: $r_1 \times r_2 = 2a$

When you eliminate a, you will get $r_1 r_2 = 2r_1 + 2r_2 \rightarrow r_1 r_2 - 2r_1 - 2r_2 = 0$

Now factor for this special equation. $r_1(r_2 - 2) - 2(r_2 - 2) = 4 \rightarrow (r_1 - 2)(r_2 - 2) = 4$

We know that $(r_1 - 2)$ and $(r_2 - 2)$ are integers.

Possible integers are as follows.

$$
\begin{array}{ccccc}
(r_1 - 2) & \times & (r_2 - 2) & = & 4 \\
1 & \times & 4 & \rightarrow r_1 = 3, \ r_2 = 6 & \rightarrow a = 3 + 6 = 9 \\
2 & \times & 2 & \rightarrow r_1 = 4, \ r_2 = 4 & \rightarrow a = 4 + 4 = 8 \\
-1 & \times & -4 & \rightarrow r_1 = 1, \ r_2 = -2 & \rightarrow a = 1 - 2 = -1 \\
-2 & \times & -2 & \rightarrow r_1 = 0, \ r_2 = 0 & \rightarrow a = 0 + 0 = 0
\end{array}
$$

Therefore, sum of values of $a = 9 + 8 + (-1) + 0 = 16$. The answer is (C).

14. For two-digit number ab $\rightarrow$ $10a+b=a+b^2$ $\rightarrow$ $9a=b^2-b$ $\rightarrow$ $a=\dfrac{b(b-1)}{9}$

To have positive integer a, the value b should be 9.
Therefore, $a=8$ and $b=9$. The two digit-number is 89. The answer is (B).

---

22 | Absolute Value Equation

1. $|x-6|=2x+8$, Piecewise function is

$$|x-6|=\begin{cases} x\geq 6, \ x-6=2x+8 \rightarrow x=-14 \ \text{(False)} \\ x<6, \ -x+6=2x+8 \rightarrow 3x=-2 \rightarrow x=-\dfrac{2}{3} \ \text{(OK)} \end{cases}$$

Therefore, the solution is $x=-\dfrac{2}{3}$.

2. $\big|2x-|10-2x|\big|=x$

If $x\geq 5$, then $|2x+10-2x|=x \rightarrow |10|=x \rightarrow x=10$ (OK)

If $x<5$, then $|2x-10+2x|=x \rightarrow |4x-10|=x$. Now apply pricewise function again.

$$|4x-10|=x\begin{cases} \text{If } x\geq \dfrac{5}{2}, \text{ then } 4x-10=x \rightarrow 3x=10 \rightarrow x=\dfrac{10}{3}:\text{Satistify } \dfrac{5}{2}<\dfrac{10}{3}<5 \\ \text{If } x<\dfrac{5}{2}, \text{ then } -4x+10=x \rightarrow x=2:\text{Satisfy } 2<\dfrac{5}{2}. \end{cases}$$

Therefore, the solution is $x=10, \dfrac{10}{3},$ and 2.

3. $x=\big|2x-|60-2x|\big|$?

If $x\geq 30$, then $|2x+60-2x|=x \rightarrow |60|=x \rightarrow x=60$ (OK)

If $x<30$, then $|2x-60+2x|=x \rightarrow |4x-60|=x$. Now apply pricewise function again.

$$|4x-60|=x\begin{cases} \text{If } x\geq 15, \text{ then } 4x-60=x \rightarrow 3x=60 \rightarrow x=20:\text{Satistify } 15<20<30 \\ \text{If } x<15, \text{ then } -4x+60=x \rightarrow 5x=60 \rightarrow x=12:\text{Satisfy } 12<15. \end{cases}$$

Therefore, the solution is $x=60, 20,$ and 12. Therefore, $60+20+12=92$. The answer is (C).

4. $\sqrt{5|x|+8}=\sqrt{x^2-16}$ $\rightarrow$ You can see that domain is $x^2-16\geq 0 \rightarrow x\leq -4$ or $x\geq 4$.

$\sqrt{5|x|+8}=\sqrt{x^2-16} \rightarrow 5|x|+8=x^2-16 \rightarrow x^2-5|x|-24=0$

$$x^2-5|x|-24=0\begin{cases} \text{If } x\geq 0, \text{ then } x^2-5x-24=0 \rightarrow (x-8)(x+3)=0 \rightarrow x=8 \\ \text{If } x<0, \text{ then } x^2+5x-24=0 \rightarrow (x+8)(x-3)=0 \rightarrow x=-8 \end{cases}$$

Therefore, $(-8)(8)=-64$. The answer is (A).

23	Discriminant

1. In order not to have distinct real roots, discriminant should be $D \leq 0$.

$b^2 - 4c \leq 0$ and $c^2 - 4b \leq 0$

Since $b, c > 0$,

$b^2 - 4c \leq 0 \rightarrow c \geq \frac{1}{4}b^2$ and $c^2 - 4b \leq 0 \rightarrow c^2 \leq 4b \rightarrow c \leq 2\sqrt{b}$

The graphs are as follows.

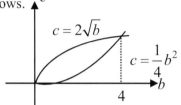

Find the integer value of y at points $b = 1, 2, 3$

At $b = 1 \rightarrow \frac{1}{4} \leq c \leq 2 \rightarrow c = 1, 2 \; (2\text{point})$

At $b = 2 \rightarrow 1 \leq c \leq 2\sqrt{2} \rightarrow 1, 2 \; (2\text{points})$

At $b = 3 \rightarrow \frac{9}{4} \leq c \leq 2\sqrt{3} \rightarrow 2.25 \leq c \leq 3.3 \rightarrow c = 3 \; (1\text{point})$

At $b = 4 \rightarrow (1 \text{ point of intersection})$

Therefore, total number of points is $2 + 2 + 1 + 1 = 6$. The answer is (B).

24	Simplifying Complex Radical

1. $\sqrt{9 - 6\sqrt{2}} + \sqrt{9 + 6\sqrt{2}} = \sqrt{(6+3) - 2\sqrt{18}} + \sqrt{(6+3) + 2\sqrt{18}} = \sqrt{6} - \sqrt{3} + \sqrt{6} + \sqrt{3} = 2\sqrt{6}$

The answer is (B).

2. $\sqrt{18 - 8\sqrt{2}} + \sqrt{38 + 12\sqrt{2}} = \sqrt{(16+2) - 2\sqrt{32}} + \sqrt{(36+2) + 2\sqrt{72}} =$

$(\sqrt{16} - \sqrt{2}) + (\sqrt{36} + \sqrt{2}) = 10$

The answer is (E).

3. $\sqrt{12 - 8\sqrt{2}} - \sqrt{12 + 8\sqrt{2}} = \sqrt{(8+4) - 2\sqrt{32}} - \sqrt{(8+4) + 2\sqrt{32}} = (\sqrt{8} - \sqrt{4}) - (\sqrt{8} + \sqrt{4}) = -4$

$|-4| = 4$. The answer is (A).

25	Sum of Digits of a Number

1. $N = \sqrt{25^{64} \cdot 64^{25}} = \sqrt{5^{128} \cdot 2^{150}} = 5^{64} \cdot 2^{75} = (5 \cdot 2)^{64} \cdot 2^{11} = 2048 \times 10^{64}$

Sum of the digits is $2 + 0 + 4 + 8 = 14$.

2. $N = 2^{30} \cdot 2^{16} \cdot 5^{50} = 2^{46} \cdot 5^{46} \cdot 5^4 = (2 \cdot 5)^{46} \cdot 5^4 = 625 \times 10^{46}$

Sum of digits is $6+2+5=13$. The answer is (D).

---

26 | How to solve $ax + by = c$?

1. Set up the equation. $2x + 3y = 2016$

$$y = \frac{2016 - 2x}{3} \rightarrow y = \frac{2(1008 - x)}{3} \rightarrow 1008 - x \equiv 0 \bmod 3$$

Since $1008 \equiv 0 \bmod 3$, we can say that $x \equiv 0 \bmod 3$. $x \in [0, 1008]$

Therefore, the number of x is $\left\lfloor \dfrac{1008}{3} \right\rfloor + 1 = 337$. The answer is (C).

2. Set up the equation. $3x + 4y = 2016$

$$y = \frac{2016 - 3x}{4} \rightarrow y = \frac{2(672 - x)}{4} \rightarrow 672 - x \equiv 0 \bmod 4$$

Since $672 \equiv 0 \bmod 4$, we can say that $x \equiv 0 \bmod 4$. $x \in [0, 672]$

Therefore, the number of x is $\left\lfloor \dfrac{672}{4} \right\rfloor + 1 = 169$. The answer is (A).

3. Set up the equation. $2x + 5y = 2020$

$$y = \frac{2020 - 2x}{5} = \frac{2(1010 - x)}{5} \rightarrow 1010 - x \equiv 0 \bmod 5$$

Since $1010 \equiv 0 \bmod 5$, we can say that $x \equiv 0 \bmod 5$.

$x \in [5, 1005]$ because at $x \neq 0$ and $x \neq 1010 \rightarrow y = 0$

Therefore, the number of x is $\left\lfloor \dfrac{1005}{5} \right\rfloor = 201$. The answer is (B).

---

27 | Vistas' Formulas

1. We know that $\alpha^2 + \beta^2 = (\alpha + \beta)^2 - 2\alpha\beta$, $\alpha + \beta = -5$, and $\alpha\beta = -3$.

Therefore, $\alpha^2 + \beta^2 = (-5)^2 - 2(-3) = 31$.

2. $\dfrac{1}{r_1} + \dfrac{1}{r_2} = \dfrac{r_1 + r_2}{r_1 r_2}$ and $r_1 + r_2 = 7$, $r_1 r_2 = -10$. Therefore, $\dfrac{1}{r_1} + \dfrac{1}{r_2} = \dfrac{7}{-10} = -\dfrac{7}{10}$

3. We can see

164

$$\begin{cases} \alpha^3 + \beta^3 = (\alpha + \beta)(\alpha^2 - \alpha\beta + \beta^2) \\ \alpha^2 + \beta^2 = (\alpha + \beta)^2 - 2\alpha\beta \\ \alpha + \beta = 8, \quad \alpha\beta = 11 \end{cases} \rightarrow \begin{cases} \alpha + \beta = 8, \quad \alpha\beta = 11 \\ \alpha^2 + \beta^2 = 8^2 - 2(11) = 42 \\ \alpha^3 + \beta^3 = (8)(42 - 11) = 248 \end{cases}$$

Therefore, $(\alpha^3 + \beta^3) + (\alpha^2 + \beta^2) + (\alpha + \beta) = 248 + 42 + 8 = 298$.

4. We know that $r_1 + r_2 + r_3 = 2$ and $r_1r_2 + r_2r_3 + r_3r_1 = 5$.

$$r_1^2 + r_2^2 + r_3^2 = (r_1 + r_2 + r_3)^2 - 2(r_1r_2 + r_2r_3 + r_3r_1) = (2)^2 - 2(5) = -6$$

5. $(2x+3)(x-4) + (2x+3)(x-6) = 0 \rightarrow (2x+3)(2x-10) = 0 \rightarrow x = -\dfrac{3}{2}, x = 5$

Therefore, $-\dfrac{3}{2} + 5 = \dfrac{7}{2}$. Or you also can use Vieta's formula.

$(2x+3)(x-4) + (2x+3)(x-6) = 0 \rightarrow 4x^2 - 14x - 30 = 0 \rightarrow$ Sum of the roots $= -\left(\dfrac{-14}{4}\right) = \dfrac{7}{2}$

6. From $\alpha + \beta = 63$ and $\alpha\beta = k$, only $\alpha = 2, \beta = 61$ satisfy the constraint, because sum of two primes except 2 is even number. Therefore, there will be only one value of $k = 122$. Answer is (B).

7. We got $d + e = -\dfrac{3}{2}$ and $de = -\dfrac{5}{2}$. Now $(d-1)(e-1) = de - (d+e) + 1 = -\dfrac{5}{2} - \left(-\dfrac{3}{2}\right) + 1 = 0$.

Answer is (B).

8. Roots of $(x^2 - 2x + 2)$: $1 + i$ and $1 - i$ $\rightarrow$ Two distinct roots

Roots of $(x^2 - 4x + 8)$: $2 + 2i$ and $2 - 2i$ $\rightarrow$ Two distinct roots

We already got four distinct roots. Therefore, the roots of $(x^2 - cx + 4)$ should be same as two of them but, their product is 4 (by Vieta's formula). So, the roots are:

$\qquad\qquad 1 + i$ and $2 - 2i$ $\quad$ or $\quad 1 - i$ and $2 + 2i$ $\rightarrow$ Their product is 4.

We know that sum of the roots is C. $(1+i) + (2-2i) = 3 - i$ or $(1-i) + (2+2i) = 3 + i$

So, $|C| = |3 - i| = |3 + i| = \sqrt{10}$. Answer is (E).

9. We can see $s^3 - 22s^2 + 80s - 67 = (s-p)(s-q)(s-r)$ because p, q, r are the roots. Now we have

$$\dfrac{1}{s^3 - 22s^2 + 80s - 67} = \dfrac{A}{s-p} + \dfrac{B}{s-q} + \dfrac{C}{s-r} = \dfrac{A(s-q)(s-r) + B(s-p)(s-r) + C(s-p)(s-q)}{(s-p)(s-q)(s-r)} .$$

$$\dfrac{1}{s^3 - 22s^2 + 80s - 67} = \dfrac{A(s-q)(s-r) + B(s-p)(s-r) + C(s-p)(s-q)}{(s-p)(s-q)(s-r)}$$

Finally, we got

$1 = A(s-q)(s-r) + B(s-p)(s-r) + C(s-p)(s-q)$

Now plug-in numbers.

If $s = p$, then $1 = A(p-q)(p-r)$.

If $s = q$, then $1 = B(q-p)(q-r)$.

If $s = r$, then $1 = C(r-p)(r-q)$.

Therefore, $\dfrac{1}{A} = (p-q)(p-r)$, $\dfrac{1}{B} = (q-p)(q-r)$, and $\dfrac{1}{C} = (r-p)(r-q)$.

$\dfrac{1}{A} + \dfrac{1}{B} + \dfrac{1}{C} = (p-q)(p-r) + (q-p)(q-r) + (r-p)(r-q) = (p^2+q^2+r^2) - (pq+qr+rp)$

That is

$\dfrac{1}{A} + \dfrac{1}{B} + \dfrac{1}{C} == (p+q+r)^2 - 3(pq+qr+rp)$

We know that $p+q+r = 22$ and $pq+qr+rp = 80$. Therefore,

$\dfrac{1}{A} + \dfrac{1}{B} + \dfrac{1}{C} = (22)^2 - 3(80) = 244$.　Answer is (B).

10. Product of the roots $= 2010 = 2 \times 3 \times 5 \times 67$

To have smallest value of a, three roots should be $(5), (2 \times 3)$, and (67). Therefore, the smallest value of a is $5 + 6 + 67 = 78$. Answer is (A).

11. By Vieta's formula, $\left(a + \dfrac{1}{b}\right)\left(b + \dfrac{1}{a}\right) = q \rightarrow ab + 1 + 1 + \dfrac{1}{ab} = q$

We can see $ab = 2$. Therefore, $q = 2 + 1 + 1 + \dfrac{1}{2} = \dfrac{9}{2}$.　The answer is (D).

12. $S = \dfrac{1}{r_1} + \dfrac{1}{r_2} = \dfrac{r_1 + r_2}{r_1 \cdot r_2}$

$\dfrac{2003}{2004} x + 1 + \dfrac{1}{x} = 0 \rightarrow \dfrac{2003}{2004} x^2 + x + 1 = 0$　and $r_1 + r_2 = -\dfrac{2004}{2003}$　and $r_1 \cdot r_2 = \dfrac{2004}{2003}$

Therefore, $S = \dfrac{r_1 + r_2}{r_1 \cdot r_2} = \dfrac{-2004/2003}{2004/2003} = -1$. The answer is (B).

---

28 | LCM and GCF

1. $40 \times m = \gcd \times \text{lcm} \rightarrow 40m = 10 \times 280 \rightarrow m = 70$

2. $18 \times k = 450 \times 6 \rightarrow k = 150$　The other number is 150.

3. Define $a = 40k_1$ and $b = 40k_2$, where k_1 and k_2 are relatively prime.

$k_1 k_2 = 1600 \div 40 = 40$

Therefore, $(k_1, k_2) = (1, 40), (5, 8), (8, 5)(40, 1)$　4 pairs available

So, $(a, b) = (40k_1, 40k_2) \rightarrow (40, 1600), (200, 320), (320, 200), (40, 1600)$

The answer is (E).

4. Let $x = \text{lcm}(a, b)$, $y = \gcd(a, b)$. We know $ab = xy$ and $x > y$.

Now the equation is

$xy + 63 = 20x + 12y \rightarrow xy - 20x - 12y = -63 \rightarrow x(y-20) - 12(y-20) = 240 - 63$

$(x-12)(y-20) = 177 \rightarrow$　There are two different combinations as follows.

166

$$\begin{cases} x - 12 = 177 \\ y - 20 = 1 \end{cases} \text{ or } \begin{cases} x - 12 = 59 \\ y - 20 = 3 \end{cases} \rightarrow \text{ Solutions are } \begin{cases} x = 189 \\ y = 21 \end{cases} \text{ and } \begin{cases} x = 71 \\ y = 23 \end{cases}$$

Remember: $\mathrm{lcm}(a,b)$ is a multiple of $\gcd(a,b)$. The only solution is $\begin{cases} x = \mathrm{lcm}(a,b) = 189 \\ y = \gcd(a,b) = 21 \end{cases}$.

Therefore, (a,b) must be $\dfrac{21|a \quad b}{1 \quad 9}$ or $\dfrac{21| a \quad b}{9 \quad 1}$. $\rightarrow (21,189),(189,\,21)$

The answer is (B).

5. We know that 63 and $n+120$ multiples of 21, and $n+63$ and 120 are multiples of 60.

Therefore, $n+120 \equiv 0 \bmod 21$ (63 is already $0 \equiv \bmod 3$) and $n+63 \equiv 0 \bmod 60$.

From these two,

$$\begin{cases} \text{Since } 120 \equiv -6 \bmod 21 \rightarrow n \equiv 6 \bmod 21 \\ \text{Since } 63 \equiv 3 \bmod 60 \rightarrow n \equiv -3 \bmod 60 \end{cases} \rightarrow \begin{cases} n \equiv 237 \bmod 21 \\ n \equiv 237 \bmod 60 \end{cases} \rightarrow n \equiv 237 \bmod 420$$

Case 1) $n = 657$

$\dfrac{21|63 \quad 777}{3 \quad 37}$ $\rightarrow$ 3 and 37 are relatively prime (OK)

$\dfrac{60|720 \quad 120}{12 \quad 2}$ are not relatively prime (Not working)

Keep continuing until we find a correct. (Next numbers 1077, 1497 are still not working) Now the next number, 1917.

$\dfrac{21|63 \quad 2037}{3 \quad 97}$ and $\dfrac{60|1980 \quad 120}{33 \quad 2}$ are both relatively prime.

Therefore, the least integer is 1917, and $1+9+1+7 = 18$. The answer is (C).

2 9 | Modular Arithmetic

1. Using Modulo N, we can see that $47 \equiv r \bmod N$ and $25 \equiv r \bmod N$. Now from theorem 5 with the same modulo N, $\rightarrow 47 - 25 \equiv (r - r) \bmod N \rightarrow 22 \equiv 0 \bmod N$. N can be 2,11, or 22. Therefore, the largest number is 22.

2. Modulo N will be applied so that $37 \equiv r \bmod N$ and $54 \equiv 2r \bmod N$.

$$\begin{cases} 37 \equiv r \bmod N \rightarrow 74 \equiv 2r \bmod N \text{ (Mulyiplied by 2)} \\ 54 \equiv 2r \bmod N \rightarrow 54 \equiv 2r \bmod N \end{cases}$$

From Theorem 5, $74 - 54 \equiv (2r - 2r) \bmod N \rightarrow 20 \equiv 0 \bmod N$.

N can be positive divisors of 20, and the largest value of N is 20.

3. From theorem 3,

If $\begin{cases} N \equiv 2 \bmod 3 \\ N \equiv 2 \bmod 4 \\ N \equiv 2 \bmod 6 \\ N \equiv 2 \bmod 7 \end{cases}$, then $N \equiv 2 \bmod 84$ where, $84 = lcm(3,4,6,7)$

Therefore, the least number is $84 + 2 = 86$.

4. From the given,

If $\begin{cases} N \equiv 1 \bmod 2 \\ N \equiv 2 \bmod 3 \\ N \equiv 3 \bmod 4 \\ N \equiv 4 \bmod 5 \end{cases}$, then $\begin{cases} N+1 \equiv 2 \bmod 2 \\ N+1 \equiv 3 \bmod 3 \\ N+1 \equiv 4 \bmod 4 \\ N+1 \equiv 5 \bmod 5 \end{cases} \rightarrow \begin{cases} N+1 \equiv 0 \bmod 2 \\ N+1 \equiv 0 \bmod 3 \\ N+1 \equiv 0 \bmod 4 \\ N+1 \equiv 0 \bmod 5 \end{cases} \rightarrow N+1 \equiv 0 \bmod 60.$

where, $60 = lcm(2,3,4,5)$.

Therefore, the least number of $N+1$ is 60. $N = 59$.

5.

$\begin{cases} 171 \equiv 80 \bmod n \\ 468 \equiv 13 \bmod n \end{cases} \rightarrow \begin{cases} 171-80 \equiv 0 \bmod n \\ 468-13 \equiv 0 \bmod n \end{cases} \rightarrow \begin{cases} 91 \equiv 0 \bmod n \\ 455 \equiv 0 \bmod n \end{cases}$

We know that $0 < n \le 91$ and n must be common divisors of 91 and 455.

We got $n = 7, 13, 91$. Therefore, $7 + 13 + 91 = 111$.

6. $n \equiv 42 \bmod 2016 \rightarrow n \equiv 42 \bmod (24 \times 84)$ From theorem 2,

$n \equiv 42 \bmod (24 \times 84) \rightarrow n \equiv 42 \bmod 24 \rightarrow n \equiv 18 \bmod 24$. The remainder is 18.

7. From theorem 5,

$\begin{cases} m \equiv 2 \bmod 7 \\ n \equiv 6 \bmod 7 \end{cases} \rightarrow m \times n \equiv (2 \times 6) \bmod 7 \rightarrow m \times n \equiv 12 \bmod 7 \rightarrow m \times n \equiv 5 \bmod 7$

The remainder is 5.

8.

$\begin{cases} a \equiv 2 \bmod 7 \\ b \equiv 3 \bmod 7 \end{cases} \rightarrow a \times b \equiv (2 \times 3) \bmod 7 \rightarrow a \times b \equiv 6 \bmod 7 \rightarrow a \times b \equiv -1 \bmod 7$

$(a \times b) + 1 \equiv 0 \bmod 7$. the largest number of multiple 7 is 994. Therefore, $a \times b = 993$.

9. Using theorem 2,

$\begin{cases} n \equiv 2 \bmod 6 \\ n \equiv 3 \bmod 7 \end{cases}$ (add 4) $\rightarrow \begin{cases} n+4 \equiv 6 \bmod 6 \\ n+4 \equiv 7 \bmod 7 \end{cases} \rightarrow \begin{cases} n+4 \equiv 0 \bmod 6 \\ n+4 \equiv 0 \bmod 7 \end{cases} \rightarrow n+4 \equiv 0 \bmod 42,$

where $42 = lcm(6,7)$. Therefore, $n+4 =$ multiples of 42.

$n = 38, 80, \cdots$ (First term is 38 with common difference $d = 42$): Arithmetic progression.

$S = \dfrac{(a_1 + a_n)n}{2} \rightarrow a_n = 38 + (n-1)42 \le 1000 \rightarrow n = 23$ and $a_{23} = 38 + (23-1)42 = 962$

Therefore, $S = \dfrac{(38+962)23}{2} = 11,500$.

10. Using theorem 4,

$$\begin{cases} a \equiv 2 \bmod 7 \\ b \equiv 1 \bmod 7 \end{cases} \rightarrow \begin{cases} a^2 \equiv 2^2 \bmod 7 \\ b \equiv 1 \bmod 7 \end{cases} \rightarrow a^2 + b \equiv (4+1) \bmod 7 \rightarrow a^2 + b \equiv 5 \bmod 7$$

Therefore, the remainder is 5.

11. Using theorem 5,

$$\begin{cases} 618 \equiv r \bmod d \\ 343 \equiv r \bmod d \\ 277 \equiv r \bmod d \end{cases} \rightarrow \begin{cases} 618 - 343 \equiv 0 \bmod d \\ 343 - 277 \equiv 0 \bmod d \end{cases} \rightarrow \begin{cases} 275 \equiv 0 \bmod d \\ 66 \equiv 0 \bmod d \end{cases} \rightarrow 275 - 4(65) \equiv 0 \bmod d$$

$$\rightarrow 11 \equiv 0 \bmod d$$

Therefore, $d = 11$.

12. $$\begin{cases} n^2 \equiv 4 \bmod 5 \\ n^3 \equiv 2 \bmod 5 \end{cases} \rightarrow \begin{cases} n^2 \cdot n \equiv 4n \bmod 5 \\ n^3 \equiv 2 \bmod 5 \end{cases} \rightarrow (\text{If } n = 3, 8, \cdots) \begin{cases} n^3 \equiv 12 \bmod 5 \\ n^3 \equiv 2 \bmod 5 \end{cases} \rightarrow \begin{cases} n^3 \equiv 2 \bmod 5 \\ n^3 \equiv 2 \bmod 5 \end{cases}$$

Therefore, $3 \equiv 3 \bmod 5$, or $8 \equiv 3 \bmod 5 \cdots$. Remainder should be 3.

13. $n \equiv 5 \bmod 7 \rightarrow 5n \equiv 25 \bmod 7 \rightarrow 5n \equiv (25 - 21) \bmod 7 \rightarrow 5n \equiv 4 \bmod 7 \rightarrow r = 4$

14.

$$\begin{cases} n \equiv 1 \bmod 7 \\ n \equiv 3 \bmod 5 \end{cases} \rightarrow \begin{cases} n \equiv (1+7) \bmod 7 \\ n \equiv (3+5) \bmod 5 \end{cases} \rightarrow \begin{cases} n \equiv 8 \bmod 7 \\ n \equiv 8 \bmod 5 \end{cases},$$

$$\rightarrow n - 8 \equiv 0 \bmod 35, \text{ where } 35 = lcm(7, 5).$$

Largest multiple of 35 is 980. Therefore, $n = 980 + 8 = 988$.

15.

$$\begin{cases} n \equiv 4 \bmod 7 \\ n \equiv 3 \bmod 9 \end{cases} \rightarrow \begin{cases} n \equiv 39 \bmod 7 \\ n \equiv 39 \bmod 9 \end{cases} \rightarrow n \equiv 39 \bmod 63, \text{ where } 63 = lcm(7, 9)$$

Therefore, the smallest value of n is $63 \times 0 + 39 = 39$.

16. Difference between the two Tuesdays is $(365 - 300) + 200 = 256$. But $265 \equiv -1 \bmod 7 \rightarrow$ Monday.

In order to have the same date, year N must be a leap year. Year $N - 1$ is not a leap year.

$(366 - 300) + 200 = 266 \rightarrow 266 \equiv 0 \bmod 7$. Now the difference between the 100th day of year $N - 1$

and the 300th day of year N is $(365 - 100) + 300 = 565$.

$565 \equiv 5 \bmod 7$ or $565 \equiv -2 \bmod 7$. Five days before Tuesday is Thursday. The answer is (A).

17. For number to have a unit digit 1, $N \equiv 1 \bmod 10$ is required. $(k = \text{integer})$

Sample space: $5 \times 20 = 100$ numbers

1) $11 \equiv 1 \bmod 10 \rightarrow 11^k \equiv 1 \bmod 10 \rightarrow k = 1999 \cdots 2018 \Rightarrow 20$ numbers

2) $13^4 \equiv 1 \bmod 10 \rightarrow 13^{4k} \equiv 1 \bmod 10 \rightarrow 4k = 2000, 2004 \cdots 2016 \Rightarrow 5$ numbers

3) $15^k \equiv 5 \bmod 10 \rightarrow$ unit digit is 5.

4) $17^4 \equiv 1 \bmod 10 \rightarrow 17^{4k} \equiv 1 \bmod 10 \rightarrow 4k = 2000, 2004, \cdots 2016 \Rightarrow 5$ numbers

5) $19^2 \equiv 1 \bmod 10 \rightarrow 19^{2k} \equiv 1 \bmod 10 \rightarrow 2k = 2000, 2002, \cdots 2018 \Rightarrow 10$ numbers

Therefore, $P = \dfrac{20+5+5+10}{100} = \dfrac{40}{100} = \dfrac{2}{5}$. The answer is (E).

18. We can see that the first 2018 numbers can be expressed as follows.

$10^2 + 1, \ 10^3 + 1, \ 10^4 + 1, \ \cdots, \ 10^{2019} + 1 \ \rightarrow \ 10^k + 1$, where $k = 2, 3, 4, \cdots 2019$

$10^k + 1 = 0 \bmod 101 \ \rightarrow \ 10^k \equiv -1 \bmod 101$

Now we know that $100^1 \equiv -1 \bmod 101 \ \rightarrow \ 100^3 \equiv -1 \bmod 101 \ \rightarrow \ 100^5 \equiv -1 \bmod 101 \cdots$

or, $\left(10^2, 10^6, 10^{10}, \cdots 10^{2018}\right) \equiv -1 \bmod 101$

Therefore, $\dfrac{2018-2}{4} + 1 = 505$ numbers. The answer is (C).

19. From theorem 7,

If $n \equiv r \bmod 6$, then $n^3 \equiv r \bmod 6$.

If $a_1 + a_2 + \cdots + a_{2018} \equiv r \bmod 6$, then $a_1^3 + a_2^3 + \cdots + a_{2018}^3 \equiv r \bmod 6$.

Now $2018 \equiv 2 \bmod 6 \ \rightarrow \ 2018^2 \equiv 4 \bmod 6 \ \rightarrow \ 2018^3 \equiv 2 \bmod 6 \ \rightarrow \ 2018^4 \equiv 4 \bmod 6$.

We can see it is periodic mode. Therefore, $2018^{2018} \equiv 4 \bmod 6$. Remainder is 4.
The answer is (E).

20. From theorem 8,

"$S(1507) = 13$" means "$1507 \equiv 13 \bmod 9$".

So, "$S(n) = 1274$" means "$n \equiv 1274 \bmod 9$. That is $n \equiv 5 \bmod 9$.

$n + 1 \equiv (5+1) \bmod 9 \ \rightarrow \ n+1 \equiv 6 \bmod 9$

Only $1239 \equiv 15 \bmod 9 \ \rightarrow \ 6 \bmod 9$. Answer is (D).

21. From $13 \equiv 1 \bmod 10 \ \rightarrow \ 13^4 \equiv 1^4 \bmod 10, \ 13^{2000} = \left(13^4\right)^{500} \equiv 1 \bmod 10$

We still have $13^3 \ \rightarrow \ 13^3 \equiv 7 \bmod 10$. Therefore, $13^{2003} = 13^{2000} \cdot 13^4 \equiv (1)(7) \bmod 10$
Answer is (C).

22. We know that $10!, 11!, 12!, \cdots, 2016!$ are divisible by 100 and tens digits are all 0.

We just check tens digit of $(7! + 8! + 9!)$. $7! + 8! + 9! = 7!(1 + 8 + 72) = 5040 \times 81 \equiv 40 \pmod{100}$
There for tens digit of the number is 4. Answer is (C)

23. From $3^0 \equiv 1 \bmod 8, \ 3^1 \equiv 3 \bmod 8, \ 3^2 \equiv 1 \bmod 8,$ and $3^3 \equiv 3 \bmod 8,$ we can see that

$\left(3^0 + 3^1 + 3^2 + 3^3\right) \equiv (1+3+1+3) \bmod 8 \equiv 0 \bmod 8$. The series is in periodic mode as follows.

$3^4 \equiv 1 \bmod 8 \qquad\qquad 3^8 \equiv 1 \bmod 8$

$3^5 \equiv 3 \bmod 8 \qquad\qquad 3^9 \equiv 3 \bmod 8$

$\qquad\qquad\qquad \rightarrow 0 \bmod 8 \qquad\qquad\qquad \rightarrow 0 \bmod 8 \cdots$

$3^6 \equiv 1 \bmod 8 \qquad\qquad 3^{10} \equiv 1 \bmod 8$

$3^7 \equiv 3 \bmod 8 \qquad\qquad 3^{11} \equiv 3 \bmod 8$

Now, 3^{2009} is 2010th term. Up to 2008 terms, the series is $0 \bmod 8$. Two more terms 2008 and 2009 have remainder 1 and 3. Therefore the remainder is $1+3=4$. Answer is (D).

24. From seven days, we can see modulo 7 periodic mode.

Su	M	T	W	Th	Fr	Sa	
0	1	2	3	4	5	6	$\rightarrow$ mod 7

From the table, 2008, May 27 is 2 mod7. Now we can see that 365 days $\equiv 1 \bmod 7$ and 366 days $\equiv 2 \bmod 7$. (2012 and 2016 are leap years)

For every 365 days: the birth date moves **one day forward**, and for 366 days: the birthdate moves **two days forward**. therefore, the birthdate will change as follows.

$$\begin{bmatrix} 2009 & \rightarrow & \text{Wednesday} \\ 2010 & \rightarrow & \text{Thursday} \\ 2011 & \rightarrow & \text{Friday} \\ 2012 & \rightarrow & \text{Sunday (leap year)} \\ 2013 & \rightarrow & \text{Monday} \end{bmatrix} \begin{bmatrix} 2014 & \rightarrow & \text{Tuesday} \\ 2015 & \rightarrow & \text{Wednesday} \\ 2016 & \rightarrow & \text{Friday (leap year)} \\ 2017 & \rightarrow & \text{Saturday} \end{bmatrix}$$

The answer is (E).

25. All 2010 integers are grouped as follows.

1(mod 3)	2(mod3)	0(mod3)
1	2	3
4	5	6
7	8	9
$\vdots$	$\vdots$	$\vdots$
2008	2009	2010

First column numbers are all 1(mod 3) $\rightarrow$ Reminder 1 when divided by 3.

Second column numbers are 2(mod 3) and third column numbers are 0(mod 3)

Now we can see that $abc + ab + a = a(bc + b + 1)$.

Case 1) If $a \equiv 0 \pmod 3$, the number is divisible by 3 with probability $\frac{1}{3}$.

Case 2) If $a \not\equiv 0 \pmod 3$, then $(bc + b + 1) \equiv 0 \pmod 3$, $bc + b = b(c+1) \equiv 2 \pmod 3$.

We have several cases again.

case 1) $b \equiv 0 \pmod 3$ and $c \equiv 1 \pmod 3$ $\rightarrow \left(\frac{1}{3}\right)\left(\frac{1}{3}\right) = \frac{1}{9}$

case 2) $b \equiv 1 \pmod 3$ $b \equiv 1 \pmod 3$ and $c \equiv 0 \pmod 3$ $\rightarrow \left(\frac{1}{3}\right)\left(\frac{1}{3}\right) = \frac{1}{9}$

Therefore, the total probability $= \frac{1}{3} + \frac{2}{3}\left(\frac{1}{9} + \frac{1}{9}\right) = \frac{13}{27}$. The answer is (E).

26. First, you can recognize
    1) first two numbers are odd or even to have an integer average. (sum of the first two numbers must be divisible by 2.)
    2) sum of the five numbers is 400.
    3) Sum of the four numbers is divisible by 4. There are only two cases as follows.

$$400-80=320 \text{ and } 400-76=326$$

. 4) Check the first three numbers is divisible by 3.
We can see that
$$71\equiv 2(\bmod 3),\ 76\equiv 1(\bmod 3),\ 80\equiv 2(\bmod 3),\ 82\equiv 1(\bmod 3),\ 91\equiv 1(\bmod 3)$$
If you choose 71 and 91 ($71+91\equiv 2+1(\bmod 3)\equiv 3(\bmod 3)$), you need $0(\bmod 3)$ for next number. But there is no $0(\bmod 3)$.
If you choose two even numbers 76 and 82 ($76+82\equiv 2(\bmod 3)$), then you need $1(\bmod 3)$, 71 or 91.

Case 1) If the last number is 80, list of the numbers are $76,82,91,71$.

because $76+82\equiv 2\bmod 3$ and $91\equiv 1\bmod 3$ will be next. Sum of these numbers is 400. That works.

Case 2) If the last number is 76, list of the numbers are $80,82,\cdots$

$80+82\equiv 0\bmod 3 \rightarrow$ the next number should be $0\bmod 3$. We can see that 71 and 91 are not $0\bmod 3$.

Therefore, the last number is 80. The answer is (C).

27. Four-digit number can be defined as $ab23$. To be divisible by 3, $a+b+2+3$ should be divisible by 3, which is $a+b+2+3\equiv 0\bmod 3 \rightarrow a+b\equiv -5\bmod 3 \rightarrow a+b\equiv 1\bmod 3$.

Case 1) $a\equiv 1\bmod 3$ and $b\equiv 0\bmod 3$ $\qquad a=[1,\cdots,9]$ and $b=[0,\cdots,9]$

$$a=\begin{pmatrix}1\\4\\7\end{pmatrix} \quad b=\begin{pmatrix}0\\3\\6\\9\end{pmatrix} \rightarrow 3\times 4=12$$

Case 2) $a\equiv 0\bmod 3$ and $b\equiv 1\bmod 3$ $\qquad a=[1,\cdots,9]$ and $b=[0,\cdots,9]$

$$a=\begin{pmatrix}3\\6\\9\end{pmatrix} \quad b=\begin{pmatrix}1\\4\\7\end{pmatrix} \rightarrow 3\times 3=9$$

Case 3) $a\equiv 2\bmod 3$ and $b\equiv 2\bmod 3$ $\qquad a=[1,\cdots,9]$ and $b=[0,\cdots,9]$

$$a=\begin{pmatrix}2\\5\\8\end{pmatrix} \quad b=\begin{pmatrix}2\\5\\8\end{pmatrix} \rightarrow 3\times 3=9$$

Therefore, $12+9+9=30$. The answer is (B).

28. From $\gcd(63,n+120)=21 \rightarrow n+120\equiv 0\bmod 21$ but $n+120$ is not divisible by 63.

Since $120\equiv -6\bmod 21$, $n\equiv 6\bmod 21$ but $n\not\equiv 6\bmod 63$.

From $\gcd(n+63,120)=60 \rightarrow n+63\equiv 0\bmod 60$ but $n+63$ is not divisible by 120.

Since $63\equiv 3\bmod 60$, $n\equiv -3\bmod 60$

Now $\begin{cases}n\equiv 6\bmod 21\\ n\equiv -3\bmod 60\end{cases} \rightarrow n\equiv 1077\bmod(lcm\,21,60)\ n\equiv 1077\bmod 420$

1) $n=1077 \rightarrow n+120=1197 \rightarrow$ divisible by 63 (not working)

2) $n = 1077 + 420 = 1497 \rightarrow 1497 + 63 = 1560 \rightarrow$ divisible by 120 (not working)

3) $n = 1077 + 840 = 1917 \rightarrow 1917 + 120 = 2037 \rightarrow$ not divisible by 63 (OK)

$\qquad\qquad\qquad\qquad 1917 + 63 = 1980 \rightarrow$ not divisible by 120 (OK)

Therefore, the least positive integer is 1917.

Since 1+9+1+7=18, the answer is (C).

29. $N = 27,006,000,052_9 = 2\left(9^{10}\right) + 7\left(9^9\right) + 6\left(9^6\right) + 5\left(9^1\right) + 2$

We know that $9 \equiv 4\,(\text{mod}\,5) \equiv -1\,(\text{mod}\,5)$.

Thus. $9^{10} \equiv (-1)^{10}\,\text{mod}\,5 \equiv 1\,\text{mod}\,5$, $9^9 \equiv (-1)^9\,\text{mod}\,5 \equiv -1\,\text{mod}\,5$, and so on.

In Modular 5,

$N \equiv 2(1) + 7(-1) + 6(1) + 5(-1) + 2 \equiv -2 \rightarrow -2\,\text{mod}\,5 \equiv 3\,\text{mod}\,5$

The remainder is 3. The answer is (D).

30 | Sequence and Series

1.

# of triangles	Sum of toothpicks
$a_1 = 1$	$S_1 = 3$
$a_2 = 3$	$S_2 = 3 + 6 = 3(1+2)$
$a_3 = 5$	$S_3 = 3 + 6 + 9 = 3(1+2+3)$
$\vdots$	$\vdots$
$a_{1002} = 2003$	$S_{1002} = 3(1 + 2 + 3 + \cdots + 1002)$

Since the base raw consists of 2003 equilateral triangles, the base raw is a_{1002}.

$$S_{1002} = 3(1 + 2 + 3 + \cdots + 1002) = 3\left(\frac{1 + 1002}{2}\right)1002 = 1507509. \text{ The answer is (C).}$$

2. Define three numbers in arithmetic progression as $9,\ 9 + d,\ 9 + 2d$.

Now define the numbers in geometric progression:

$\qquad\qquad 9,\quad 11 + d,\quad 29 + 2d$

By the common ratio,

$\dfrac{11 + d}{9} = \dfrac{29 + 2d}{11 + d} \rightarrow (11 + d)^2 = 9(29 + 2d) \rightarrow d^2 + 4d - 140 = 0$

$(d + 14)(d - 10) = 0 \rightarrow d = -14, d = 10$

When $d = -14$, the smallest value for the third term is $29 + 2(-14) = 1$.

The answer is (A).

3. From $a_{2^{100}}$, we need find $a_2, a_{2^2}, a_{2^3}, \cdots a_{2^{100}}$.

173

$$a_{2^1} = a_1 = 1 = 2^0$$

$$a_{2^2} = a_4 = 2a_2 = 2^{0+1}$$

$$a_{2^3} = a_8 = 4a_4 = 8 = 2^3 = 2^{0+1+2}$$

$$a_{2^4} = a_{16} = 8a_8 = 64 = 2^6 = 2^{0+1+2+3}$$

$$\vdots$$

$$a_{2^{100}} = \qquad\qquad = 2^{0+1+2+\cdots+99}$$

Therefore, $0+1+2+3+\cdots+99 = \dfrac{(0+99)100}{2} = 4950$.

The answer is 2^{4950}. The answer is (D).

---

31 | Counting Techniques

1. $[100, 999] \rightarrow$ There are 900 three-digit numbers.

    Number of multiples of $5 \rightarrow \left\lfloor \dfrac{999}{5} \right\rfloor - \left\lfloor \dfrac{99}{5} \right\rfloor = 199 - 19 = 180$

    By complementary counting, the number (not multiples of 5) $= 900 - 180 = 720$.

2. There are 900 three-digit numbers.

    Multiples of $3 = \left\lfloor \dfrac{999}{3} \right\rfloor - \left\lfloor \dfrac{99}{3} \right\rfloor = 333 - 33 = 300$, Multiples of $4 = \left\lfloor \dfrac{999}{4} \right\rfloor - \left\lfloor \dfrac{99}{4} \right\rfloor = 249 - 24 = 225$

    Multiples of $12 = \left\lfloor \dfrac{999}{12} \right\rfloor - \left\lfloor \dfrac{99}{12} \right\rfloor = 83 - 8 = 75$

    Therefore, number of multiples of 3 or 4 $= 300 + 225 - 75 = 450$.
    Now the answer is $900 - 450 = 450$.

3. The number of arrangements without restriction $= 5! = 120$.
    Now let's find the number such that boys are not next to each other.
    $$s \quad d \quad s \quad d \quad s \quad \rightarrow \quad 3! \times 2! = 12$$
    Therefore, the answer is $120 - 12 = 108$.

4. There are 900 three-digit numbers. Now find the number of three digit that doesn't have zeros.

    $\boxed{}\,\boxed{}\,\boxed{} \leftarrow$ Three-digit number

    $1 \quad 1 \quad 1$
    $2 \quad 2 \quad 2$
    $3 \quad 3 \quad 3 \quad \rightarrow 9 \times 9 \times 9 = 729$
    $\vdots \quad \vdots \quad \vdots$
    $9 \quad 9 \quad 9$

Therefore, the number of three-digit having at least one zero is $900 - 729 = 171$.

5. This question needs 1) case work 2) symmetric counting,
   Case 1: The first seat: $a \rightarrow$ Four different arrangements as follows

a	b	c		a	b	c		a	c	b		a	c	b
b	c	a		c	a	b		c	b	a		b	a	c

   Each brother-sister pair can switch each other $\rightarrow$

a	b	c

   $2 \times 2 \times 2 = 8$

   Therefore, total arrangements on this case is $4 \times 8 = 32$.

   Case 2: The first seat: b
   By symmetric counting, still 32

   Case 3: The first seat: c, still 32

   Therefore, total number is $32 \times 3 = 96$. The answer is (D).

6. Case 1) all of one kind

C	C
C	C

   $CCCC, WWWW, SSSS, PPPP \rightarrow$ 4 ways

   Case 2) 3 of a kind + 1 of a kind (3 of a kind can be C, W, S, P)

C	C
C	S, P

   $CCCS, CCCP \rightarrow 4 \times 2 = 8$ ways
   $8 \times 4 = 32$ ways

   Case 3) 2 of a kind + 2 of another kind ($CCWW, CCSS, CCPP, WWSS, WWPP, SSPP$)

C	W
W	C

   $CCWW \rightarrow 0$ way

C	C
S	S

   $CCSS \rightarrow \dfrac{4!}{2!2!} = 6$ ways

C	C
P	P

   $CCPP \rightarrow \dfrac{4!}{2!2!} = 6$ ways

   $WWSS \rightarrow 6$ ways, $WWPP \rightarrow 6$ ways $SSPP \rightarrow 0$ way
   Total 24 ways.

   Case 4) 2 of a kind + one of another + one of another
   $(CCWS, CCWP, CCSP) \; (WWCS, WWCP, WWSP) \; (SSCW, SSCP, SSWP)$
   $(PPCW, PPCS, PPWS)$
   $CCWS \rightarrow 0$ way, $CCWP \rightarrow 0$ way, $CCSP \rightarrow 4$ ways $\rightarrow$ Sub total 4 ways
   Now total $4 \times 4 = 16$ ways

Case 5) all different kind $(CWSP)$

$CWSP \rightarrow 8$ ways

C	P
S	W

$\rightarrow$ 4 ways

P	W
C	S

$\rightarrow$ 4 ways $\qquad 4+4=8$ ways

Therefore, grand total $4+32+24+16+6=84$. The answer is (C).

32	Dividing People into Groups

1. $\dbinom{12}{6}\dbinom{6}{6}\dfrac{1}{2!}=\dfrac{12!}{6!6!}\left(\dfrac{1}{2}\right)=462$

2. $\dbinom{28}{4}\dbinom{24}{12}\dbinom{12}{12}\dfrac{1}{2!}=\left(\dfrac{28!}{4!24!}\right)\left(\dfrac{24!}{12!12!}\right)\left(\dfrac{12!}{12!}\right)\dfrac{1}{2!}=\dfrac{28!}{4!\left(12!\right)^2 2!}$

3. $\dbinom{36}{6}\dbinom{30}{6}\dbinom{24}{6}\dbinom{18}{6}\dbinom{12}{6}\dbinom{6}{6}\dfrac{1}{6!}=\dfrac{36!}{\left(6!\right)^7}$

4. $\dbinom{12}{4}\dbinom{8}{4}\dbinom{4}{4}\dfrac{1}{3!}=\dfrac{12!}{\left(4!\right)^3 3!}$

5. $\dbinom{49}{7}\dbinom{42}{7}\dbinom{35}{7}\dbinom{28}{7}\dbinom{21}{7}\dbinom{14}{7}\dbinom{7}{7}\dfrac{1}{7!}=\dfrac{49!}{\left(7!\right)^8}$

6. $\dbinom{64}{8}\dbinom{56}{8}\dbinom{48}{8}\dbinom{40}{8}\dbinom{32}{8}\dbinom{24}{8}\dbinom{18}{8}\dbinom{8}{8}\dfrac{1}{8!}=\dfrac{64!}{\left(8!\right)^9}$

7. We know that $\dfrac{\left(n^2\right)!}{\left(n!\right)^{n+1}}$ is an integer, which is the number of ways to divide n^2 persons into n groups of n.

Step1) $\dfrac{\left(n^2-1\right)!}{\left(n!\right)^n}=\dfrac{n^2\left(n^2-1\right)!}{n^2\left(n!\right)^n}=\dfrac{\left(n^2\right)!}{n^2\left(n!\right)^n}$

Step2) $\dfrac{\left(n^2\right)!}{n^2\left(n!\right)^n}=\dfrac{\left(n^2\right)!}{n^2\left(n!\right)^n}\left(\dfrac{n!}{n!}\right)=\dfrac{n!\left(n^2\right)!}{n^2\left(n!\right)^{n+1}}=\dfrac{n!}{n^2}\left(\dfrac{n^2!}{\left(n!\right)^{n+1}}\right)$

Since $\dfrac{n^2!}{\left(n!\right)^{n+1}}$ is an integer, $\dfrac{n!}{n^2}=\dfrac{\left(n-1\right)!}{n}$ should be an integer.

If n is a prime, $\dfrac{\left(n-1\right)!}{n}$ cannot be an integer, and when $n=4$, it is not an integer.

There are 16 numbers that cannot produce integers as follows.

$2,3,4,5,7,11,13,17,19,23,29,31,37,41,43,47 \rightarrow 14$ numbers.

Therefore, $50-16=34$. The answer is (D).

---

33 | Counting multiples of a number

1. For the given interval $[300,900]$, the number of multiples of 7 is $\left\lfloor \dfrac{900}{7} \right\rfloor - \left\lfloor \dfrac{299}{7} \right\rfloor = 128 - 42 = 86$.

2. First, find the number of multiples of 3 or 4 as follows.

$$n(3 \text{ or } 4) = n(3) + n(4) - n(12) = \left\lfloor \dfrac{2001}{3} \right\rfloor + \left\lfloor \dfrac{2001}{4} \right\rfloor - \left\lfloor \dfrac{2001}{12} \right\rfloor = 667 + 500 - 166 = 1001$$

multiples of 3 and 5 $= \left\lfloor \dfrac{2001}{15} \right\rfloor = 133$, multiples of 4 and 5 $= \left\lfloor \dfrac{2001}{20} \right\rfloor = 100$

multiples of 3,4, and 5 $= \left\lfloor \dfrac{2001}{60} \right\rfloor = 33$

Therefore, $n(A) = 133 - 33 = 100$ and $n(A + (B + C)) = 100 + 100 = 200$.

Now the number of multiples of 3 or 4 not 5 is $1001 - 200 = 801$.   The answer is (B).

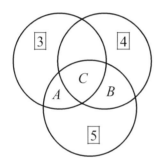

3. Let $\dfrac{n}{20-n} = k^2$. We got $n = k^2(20-n) \rightarrow n = 20k^2 - nk^2 \rightarrow n(1 + k^2) = 20k^2$.

   From $n = \dfrac{20k^2}{1 + k^2}$, we can see k^2 and $1 + k^2$ are relatively prime. It follows that $1 + k^2$ divides 20.

   For the values of $k^2 = 0,1,4,$ and 9, $n = 0,10,16,$ and 18. There are 4 numbers.
   The answer is (D).

4. From $3^8 \cdot 5^2 = a^b \rightarrow (3^4)^2 5^2 = (91 \times 5)^2 = a^b$, $a = 405$ and $b = 2$. Therefore $a + b = 407$.

   Another case: $(3^8 \cdot 5^2)^1 \rightarrow a = 164025$ and $b = 1 \rightarrow$ It's not smallest value. Answer is (D).

5. Define 2005 numbers of each set.

   Multiples of 4: $A = \{4,8,12,\cdots\cdots,8020\}$, Multiples of 6: $B = \{6,12,18,\cdots\cdots,12030\}$

   The common elements will be multiples of 12 $\rightarrow$ ($lcm(4,6) = 12$)

   Therefore, the number of multiples of 12 up to 8020 is

$$\left\lfloor \frac{8020}{12} \right\rfloor = 668.$$ The answer is (D).

6. Define $n(k) = $ number of multiple of k.

Now, $n(3 \vee 4) = n(3) + n(4) - n(3 \wedge 4) \rightarrow$

$$n(3 \vee 4) = \left\lfloor \frac{2005}{3} \right\rfloor + \left\lfloor \frac{2005}{4} \right\rfloor - \left\lfloor \frac{2005}{12} \right\rfloor = 668 + 501 - 167 = 1002$$

But this number still includes multiples of 12. We can see there are 167 multiples of 12. Therefore, $1002 - 167 = 835$. The answer is (C).

7. $n = 100q + r \rightarrow n = 99q + q + r \rightarrow 99q + q + r \equiv 0 \bmod 11$

Since $99q \equiv 0 \bmod 11$, $q + r \equiv 0 \bmod 11$

Therefore, the numbers of $n = \left\lfloor \frac{99999}{11} \right\rfloor - \left\lfloor \frac{9999}{11} \right\rfloor = 9090 - 909 = 8181$. The answer is (B).

34	How to find the largest n such that 2^n divides 100!?

1. $n = \left\lfloor \frac{100}{3} \right\rfloor + \left\lfloor \frac{100}{3^2} \right\rfloor + \left\lfloor \frac{100}{3^3} \right\rfloor + \left\lfloor \frac{100}{3^4} \right\rfloor = 33 + 11 + 3 + 1 = 48$

2. Find the largest k such that 5^k divides $100!$.

$$k = \left\lfloor \frac{100}{5} \right\rfloor + \left\lfloor \frac{100}{5^2} \right\rfloor = 20 + 4 = 24$$

Now find the largest m such that 2^m divides $100!$ You can see m is greater than k. $(5 \times 2)^{24} = 10^{24}$.

3. We realize that the number of $5's$ is equal to the number of zeros.

Ex) $\left\lfloor \dfrac{15}{5} \right\rfloor = 3 \to$ 15! have 3 zeros. $\left\lfloor \dfrac{25}{5} \right\rfloor + \left\lfloor \dfrac{25}{25} \right\rfloor = 6 \to$ 25! have 6 zeros.

$n!$	# of zeros	$2n!$	# of zeros
1!	0	2!	0
2!	0	4!	0
3!	0	6!	1
4!	0	8!	1
5!	1	10!	2
6!	1	12!	2
7!	1	14!	2
8!	1	16!	3
9!	1	18!	3
10!	2	20!	4
11!	2	22!	4
12!	2	24!	4
13!	2	26!	6
14!	2	28!	6

In the table above, at $n = 8, 9, 13, 14$, $(2n)!$ have three-time zeros of $n!$.

Therefore, $8 + 9 + 13 + 14 = 44 \to 4 + 4 = 8$. The answer is (B).

4. $a = \left\lfloor \dfrac{30}{2} \right\rfloor + \left\lfloor \dfrac{30}{2^2} \right\rfloor + \left\lfloor \dfrac{30}{2^3} \right\rfloor + \left\lfloor \dfrac{30}{2^4} \right\rfloor = 15 + 7 + 3 + 1 = 26$

$b = \left\lfloor \dfrac{30}{3} \right\rfloor + \left\lfloor \dfrac{30}{3^2} \right\rfloor + \left\lfloor \dfrac{30}{3^3} \right\rfloor = 10 + 3 + 1 = 14$

$c = \left\lfloor \dfrac{30}{5} \right\rfloor + \left\lfloor \dfrac{30}{5^2} \right\rfloor = 6 + 1 = 7$

Therefore, $a + b + c = 26 + 14 + 7 = 47$.   The answer is (C).

35 | Stars and Bars

1. Since the solution is non-negative integers, we apply theorem 2.

$n = 8$ and $k = 3$. Therefore, $\dbinom{8+3-1}{3-1} = \dbinom{10}{2} = \dfrac{10 \cdot 9}{2} = 45$

2. Since the solution is non-negative integers, we apply theorem 2.

$n = 100$ and $k = 20$. Therefore, $\dbinom{100+20-1}{19} = \dbinom{119}{19}$.

3. Since the solution is non-negative integers, we apply theorem 2.

$n = 10$ and $k = 6$. Therefore, $\dbinom{10+6-1}{6-1} = \dbinom{15}{5} = 3003$.

4. If we modify the equation, it will be equivalent to the following equation

How many nonnegative integer solutions are there to $x_1 + x_2 + x_3 + x_4 = 10$?

Since the solution is non-negative integers, we apply Ptolemy's theorem.

$n = 10$ and $k = 4$. Therefore, $\dbinom{10+4-1}{4-1} = \dbinom{13}{3} = 286$.

5. (Compare with question 2)

$n = 100$ and $k = 20$.

Since the solution is positive integers, we cannot use theorem 2.

Therefore, $\dbinom{100-1}{20-1} = \dbinom{99}{19}$.

If you want to use Ptolemy's Theorem, take out 20 for 20-kuples.

Now the question can be as follows.

What is the number of solutions in <u>non-negative integers</u> of $x_1 + x_2 + x_3 + \cdots + x_{20} = 80$?

$n = 80$ and $k = 20$. Therefore, $\dbinom{80+20-1}{20-1} = \dbinom{99}{19}$.

6. This question is not "Stars and Bars problem" because all candies are **<u>distinct.</u>**

You need to approach with a different way.

C_1	C_2	C_3	C_4	C_5	C_6	C_7
r	r	r	r	r	r	r
b	b	b	b	b	b	b
w	w	w	w	w	w	w

Each candy can go in three bags.

Total distributions is $3 \times 3 \times 3 \times 3 \times 3 \times 3 \times 3 = 3^7 = 2187$ including empty bags.

Therefore, you need to take off the numbers in which the red and blue bags are empty as follows.

C_1	C_2	C_3	C_4	C_5	C_6	C_7
0	0	0	0	0	0	0
b	b	b	b	b	b	b
w	w	w	w	w	w	w

and

C_1	C_2	C_3	C_4	C_5	C_6	C_7
r	r	r	r	r	r	r
0	0	0	0	0	0	0
w	w	w	w	w	w	w

The number of distributions is $2 \times 2 \times 2 \times 2 \times 2 \times 2 \times 2 = 2^7 = 128$

The number of distributions is $2 \times 2 \times 2 \times 2 \times 2 \times 2 \times 2 = 2^7 = 128$

These calculations include one case where the red and the blue bag are empty. (Overcount)

The answer is $2187 - (128 + 128 - 1) = 1932$. The answer is (C).

7. Keep six apples in different place for Alice, Becky and Chris. Now apply stars and bars formula. You have $24 - 6 = 18$ stars and 2 bars for dividing into three groups. Therefore, there are totally $18 + 2 = 20$ stars.

The answer is $\dbinom{20}{2} = \dfrac{20 \times 19}{2!} = 190$. Choice (C) is the answer.

8. Distribute three apples in each of the two bags, the red and blue bags. $30 - 6 = 24$ apples are now distributed into 5 bags. Now total number of stars is $24 + 4 = 28$

(24 apples + 4 bars). The answer is $\dbinom{28}{4} = 20475$.

9. You can see that there are 10 stars and 2 bars. The answer is $_{(10+2)}C_2 = {}_{12}C_2 = \dfrac{12 \cdot 11}{2!} = 66$.

   The answer is (B).

10. The number of stars is $(12-4)+3(\text{bars}) = 11$

   Therefore, $_{11}C_3 = \dfrac{11 \cdot 10 \cdot 9}{3!} = 165$. The answer is (B).

---

36 | How to distribute distinct things into different rooms.

1. Since all three bags may be empty, the number of arrangements is 3^7. The answer is (D).

c_1	c_2	c_3	c_4	c_5	c_6	c_7
A	A	A	A	A	A	A
B	B	B	B	B	B	B
C	C	C	C	C	C	C

2. The number of the case with the red bag is empty is 2^7. Therefore, the final number is $3^7 - 2^7 = 2059$. The answer is (C).

3. The number with all possible three bags are empty $= 3^7$

   The number with the red bag is empty $= 2^7$ and the number with the blue bag is empty $= 2^7$

   The number with both two bags are empty $=1$

   Therefore, the final number is $3^7 - \left(2^7 + 2^7 - 1\right) = 2187 - 128 - 128 + 1 = 1932$. The answer is (C).

---

37 | Pigeonhole Principle

1. Consider the worst case. All blue and red socks are removed.

   $bbbbbbbbbbbbrrrrrrrr\,g\,g\,\boxed{g}$ $\rightarrow 12+8+4=24$ socks

2. Consider the worst case. By taking 7 socks, we ensure that 3 socks of the same color have been taken.

   $b \quad r \quad g \quad b \quad r \quad g \quad \boxed{7}$

3. The worst case: All blue and red socks have been taken, and then 3 green socks are removed.
   $12+8+3=23$.

4. $4+1=5$ socks.

   5 socks must be drawn out of the drawer to guarantee he has a pair. In this case the pigeons are the socks he pulls out and the holes are the colors. Thus, if he pulls out 5 socks, the Pigeonhole Principle states that some two of them have the same color.

   Note the worst case that it is possible to pull out 4 socks without obtaining a pair.

5. For the difference to be a multiple of 5, the two integers must have the same remainder when divided by 5. Since there are 5 possible remainders (0-4), by the pigeonhole principle, at least two of the integers must share the same remainder. Thus, the answer is 1 (E).

Remainder when divided by 5   →   0 1 2 3 4 ?

6. By the pigeonhole principle, consider the worst case as follows

Place 532 pigeons into 12 holes. $\left\lfloor \dfrac{52}{12} \right\rfloor + 1 = 5$. The answer is (D).

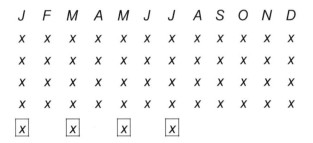

38 | How many squares does contain diagonal?

1. $y = \dfrac{10}{17}x$, where $x = 1, 2, 3, \cdots 16$. For the values of x, there is no integer value of y.

   Total points of intersection with vertical and horizontal lines is $16 + 9 = 25$.

   Therefore, the number of tiles is $25 + 1 = 26$. Answer is (C).

2. Using algebra, $y = \dfrac{12}{18}x = \dfrac{2}{3}x$ and $x \in \{1, 2, 3, \cdots 17\}$,

   At $x = 3, 6, 9, 12, 15$, y have integers.

   Points of intersection with vertical lines $= 17$ and points of intersection with horizontal lines $= 11$.

   Therefore, the number of squares crossed by the diagonal is $(17 + 11 - 5) + 1 = 24$.

   Answer is (A).

39 | How to check if a Number is Prime

1. We know that 2,4,5, and 6 cannot be in the unit's place, because they are all divisible by 2 or 5.

   2 9
   4 1   Sum of all 4 prime numbers $= 20 + 40 + 50 + 60 + (1 + 3 + 7 + 9) = 190$
   5 3
   6 7

2. We know that all prime numbers except 2 and 3 are $\pm 1 \pmod 6$ like $p = \pm 1 \pmod 6$.

   So, $p^2 = 1 \pmod 6$. Now check the numbers.

$16 \equiv -2 \pmod 6$ $24 \equiv 0 \pmod 6$ $26 \equiv 2 \pmod 6$ $96 \equiv 0 \pmod 6$

$p^2 + 16 \equiv -1 \pmod 6$ $p^2 + 24 \equiv 1 \pmod 6$ $p^2 + 26 \equiv 3 \pmod 6$ $p^2 + 96 \equiv 1 \pmod 6$

We can see that $p^2 + 26$ is not $\pm 1 \pmod 6 \rightarrow$ The number is never a prime number.

Answer is (C).

40	Base Number

1. $542_8 = 5(8^2) + 4(8) + 2 = 354$

2. $785 \div 6 = 130 R\boxed{5}$, $130 \div 6 = 21 R\boxed{4}$, $21 \div 6 = 3 R\boxed{3}$, $3 \div 6 = 0 R\boxed{3}$

   Therefore, $785 = 3345_6$.

3. $204_6 = 2(6^2) + 0(6) + 4 = 76$

   Now, $76 \div 8 = 9R\boxed{4}$, $9 \div 8 = 1R\boxed{1} \rightarrow 1 \div 8 = 0R\boxed{1}$ Therefore, $204_6 = 114_8$.

4. $\boxed{12}_3$ $\boxed{22}_3$ $\boxed{11}_3$ $\boxed{22}_3 = \boxed{1(3)+2}\boxed{2(3)+2}\boxed{1(3)+1}\boxed{2(3)+2} = 5848_9$

5. $10! = 10 \cdot 9 \cdot 8 \cdot 7 \cdot 6 \cdot 5 \cdot 4 \cdot 3 \cdot 2 \cdot 1 = (2 \cdot 5)(3^2)(2^3)7(2 \cdot 3)5(2^2)(3)(2) = 2^9 \cdot 3^4 \cdots$

   $12 = 2^2 \cdot 3 \rightarrow 10! = (2^2 \cdot 3)^4 \cdots$ $10!$ can be divided by 12 four times and creates four zeros.

6. $8! = 8 \cdot 7 \cdot 6 \cdot 5 \cdot 4 \cdot 3 \cdot 2 \cdot 1 = 2^7 \cdots = (2^3)^2 \cdots \rightarrow$ creates two zeros.

7.

   $\boxed{12}\boxed{11}\boxed{22}\boxed{11}\boxed{12}\boxed{22}\boxed{11}\boxed{11}\boxed{22}\boxed{22}_3$

   $\downarrow$

   $1(3) + 2 = 5_9$

   The first digit is 5.

8. $47_a = 74_b \rightarrow 4a + 7 = 7b + 4$ where, a and b must be greater than 7.

   $4a = 7b - 3 \rightarrow a = \dfrac{7b - 3}{4}$

   You can try $b = 8, \cdots$. If $b = 9$, then $a = 15$. Therefore, $a + b = 24$.

9. $abc_7 = cba_9$ and $a, b, c < 7$.

   $49a + 7b + c = 81c + 9b + a \rightarrow 48a = 80c + 2b \rightarrow 24a = 40c + b \rightarrow b = 8(3a - 5c)$

   Possible values of b is multiples of 8, that is $0, 8, 16, \cdots$. But $b < 7$.

   Therefore, 0 is the only value of b You can see that $a = 5$ and $c = 3$

10. The smallest 3-digit base 4 is 100_4, and the largest 3-digit base 4 is 333_4.

    $100_4 = 16$ and $333_4 = 3(16) + 3(4) + 3 = 63$. $\rightarrow 16 \le N \le 63$

The smallest 3-digit base 7 is 100_7, and the largest 3-digit base 7 is 666_7.

$100_7 = 49$ and $666_7 = 6(49) + 6(7) + 6 = 342$ → $49 \le N \le 342$

Therefore, $49 \le N \le 63$ satisfy both inequalities. There are 15 numbers.

11. When you divide the number by b, the remainder is the last digit, 3.

So, $2013 \equiv 3 \bmod b$ → $2010 \equiv 0 \bmod b$ → b must be factors of 2010.

$2010 = 2^1 \cdot 3^1 \cdot 5^1 \cdot 67^1$ → number of factors is $(1+1)(1+1)(1+1)(1+1) = 16$.

But you can see b should be greater than 3. Factors 1, 2, and 3 are not working.
Therefore, the answer is $16 - 3 = 13$.

12. The largest number 1000, find the base 16.

$1000 \div 16 = 62 R 8$, $\quad 62 \div 16 = 3 R 14$, $\quad 3 \div 16 = 0 R 3$

So, $1000 = 3E8_{16}$

Case 1) For one digit, there are 9 numbers. $\boxed{1 \sim 9}$ → 9
Case 2) For 2-digit, there are 90 numbers. $\boxed{1 \sim 9}\boxed{0 \sim 9}$ → $9 \times 10 = 90$
Case 3) For 3-digit, there are 300 numbers. $\boxed{1 \sim 3}\boxed{0 \sim 9}\boxed{0 \sim 9}$ → $3 \times 10 \times 10 = 300$
Therefore, there are $300 + 90 + 9 = 399$ numbers.
The answer is $3 + 9 + 9 = 21$.

13. We know that there are 900 three-digit numbers from 100 to 999 → $(999 - 100 + 1 = 900)$

Case 1)
   How many base-9 three-digit numbers are there?
   The smallest base-9 three-digit number is $100_9 = 1(9^2) + 0(9^1) + 0 = 81_{10}$.

   The largest base-9 three-digit number is $888_9 = 8(9^2) + 8(9) + 9 = 728_{10}$.

Case 2)
   How many base-11 three-digit numbers are there?
   The smallest base-11 three-digit number is $100_{11} = 1(11^2) + 0(11^1) + 0 = 121_{10}$.

   The largest base-11 three-digit number is $(10)(10)(10)_{11} = 10(11^2) + 10(11) + 10 = 1330_{10}$.

As you can see on the number line, there are $728 - 121 + 1 = 608$.

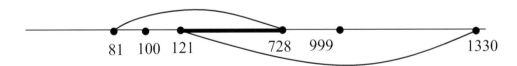

Therefore, the probability is $P = \dfrac{608}{900} \approx 0.7$. The answer is (E).

1. $0.\bar{5}_7 = \dfrac{5_7}{7-1} = \dfrac{5}{6}$ The answer is (A).

2. $0.\overline{324}_5 = \dfrac{324_5}{5^3-1} = \dfrac{3(25)+2(5)+4}{125-1} = \dfrac{89}{124}$ The answer is (E).

3. $x = 0.00\overline{31}_5 \rightarrow 5^2 x = 0.\overline{31}_5 = \dfrac{31_5}{5^2-1} = \dfrac{3(5)+1}{24} = \dfrac{16}{24} = \dfrac{2}{3}$

   Therefore, $x = \dfrac{2}{3} \times \dfrac{1}{5^2} = \dfrac{2}{75}$.

4. $x = 0.0\overline{301}_4 \rightarrow 4x = 0.\overline{301}_4 \rightarrow 4x = \dfrac{301_4}{4^3-1} = \dfrac{3(16)+0(4)+1}{63} = \dfrac{49}{63} = \dfrac{7}{9}$

   $x = \dfrac{7}{9} \times \dfrac{1}{4} = \dfrac{7}{36}$.

5. $\dfrac{7}{51} = 0.\overline{23}_k \rightarrow \dfrac{7}{51} = \dfrac{23_k}{k^2-1} = \dfrac{2k+3}{k^2-1} \rightarrow 7(k^2-1) = 102k+153 \rightarrow 7k^2-102k-160 = 0$

   $(7k+10)(k-16) = 0 \rightarrow k = 16$ (k cannot be negative).   The answer is (D).

6. $\dfrac{1}{10} = 0.0\bar{3}_k \rightarrow k\left(\dfrac{1}{10}\right) = 0.\bar{3}_k \rightarrow \dfrac{k}{10} = \dfrac{3}{k-1} \rightarrow k^2-k-30 = 0 \rightarrow (k-6)(k+5) = 0$

   Since the value of k is positive and greater than 3, $k = 6$. The answer is (C).

| 42 | Divisibility Rules |

1. By the rule 3, sum of digits should be multiple of 3.
   $9+8+a+6 = 23+a \rightarrow a = 1, 4, 7$ ($\because 0 \leq a \leq 9$)
   Actually, $9816, 9846$, and 9876 are multiples of 3.

2. Multiple of $99 \rightarrow$ divisible by 11 and divisible by 9
   We can see $0 \leq a+b \leq 18$.
   1) Divisible by 9 $\rightarrow 1+2+a+b =$ multiple of 9 $\rightarrow a+b = 6, 15$

   2) Divisible by 11 $\rightarrow 1-2+a-b = (a-b)-1 =$ multiple of 11 $\rightarrow a-b = 1$

   $\begin{cases} a+b = 6 \\ a-b = 1 \end{cases} \rightarrow a = 3.5$ and $b = 2.5$ (not ingeger $\rightarrow$ not working)

   $\begin{cases} a+b = 15 \\ a-b = 1 \end{cases} \rightarrow a = 8$ and $b = 7$

   Therefore, the number is 1287.

3. 1) We can see that $19!$ ends with three zeros.

   $\left\lfloor \dfrac{19}{5} \right\rfloor = 3 \rightarrow (5^3)(2^3) = 1000 \rightarrow H = 0$

2) $19!$ is a multiple of 9.

$1+2+1+6+T+5+1+4+M+8+3+2 = T+M+33 \rightarrow$ multiple of 9.

Therefore, $T + M = 3, 12$.

3) $19!$ is a multiple of 11.

$1-2+1-6+T-5+1-0+0-4+0-M+8-3+2-H = T-M-7$ is multiple 11.

Therefore, $T - M = -4, 7$.

Now we can see only $T + M = 12$ and $T - M = -4$ have the positive integer solution.

$\begin{cases} T + M = 12 \\ T - M = -4 \end{cases} \rightarrow T = 4$ and $M = 8$

Therefore, $T + M + H = 4 + 8 + 0 = 12$. The answer is (C).

4) $202101 \rightarrow$ Sum of the digits: 6 is divisible by 3.

$202103 \rightarrow$ Difference of the alternating sum of the digits: $4 - 4 = 0$ is a multiple of 11.

$202105 \rightarrow$ Divisible by 5.

$202107 \rightarrow$ Sum of the digits: 12 is divisible by 3.

$202109 \rightarrow$ Prime

43	Number of Subsets

1. The number of subsets is $2^8 = 256$

   The number of subsets of $\{4,6,8,9\} = 2^4 = 16 \rightarrow$ All these subsets contain only composite numbers.

   Now, using complementary counting, $256 - 16 = 240$. The answer is (D).

2. The number of subsets of $\{1,2,3,4,5,6,7,8,9,10\}$ containing 3,4, and 5 is equal to the number of subsets of $\{1,2,6,7,8,9,10\} = 2^7 = 128$. The answer is (D).

3. The number of subsets of $\{1,2,3,4,5,6,7,8\}$ containing 2 but not 3 is equal to the number of subsets of $\{1,4,5,6,7,8\} = 2^6 = 64..$ The answer is (C).

44	Greatest Integer Function (1)

1. Let $x = \lfloor x \rfloor + k$. Then $x^2 + 10000\lfloor x \rfloor = 10000(\lfloor x \rfloor + k)$. Simplify the equation.

   $x^2 = 10000k$. Since $0 \le k < 1$, $0 \le x^2 < 10000$. When you solve the inequality, we got

   $x^2 < 10000 \rightarrow (x+100)(x-100) < 0 \rightarrow -100 < x < 100$. In this range we will have

   $\lfloor x \rfloor = -99, -98, -97, \cdots -1, 0, 1, 2, 3, \cdots 99 \rightarrow 199$ numbers of $\lfloor x \rfloor$.

   Therefore, there are also 199 numbers of x, such that $-99 + k, -98 + k, \cdots, 98 + k, 99 + k$.

   The answer is (C).

2. From the domain $0 < x < 1$, we can see that $\log_2 1 = 0$, $\log_2\left(\dfrac{1}{2}\right) = -1$, $\log_2\left(\dfrac{1}{4}\right) = -2, \cdots$. It means

$$\begin{cases} \text{If } \dfrac{1}{2} \le x, y < 1, \text{ then } \log_2 x = \log_2 y = -1. \;\rightarrow\; \text{inteval is } \dfrac{1}{2} \\[2mm] \text{If } \dfrac{1}{4} \le x, y < \dfrac{1}{2}, \text{ then } \log_2 x = \log_2 y = -2. \;\rightarrow\; \text{inteval is } \dfrac{1}{4} \\[2mm] \text{If } \dfrac{1}{8} \le x, y < \dfrac{1}{4}, \text{ then } \log_2 x = \log_2 y = -3. \;\rightarrow\; \text{inteval is } \dfrac{1}{8} \\[2mm] \qquad\qquad \vdots \end{cases}$$

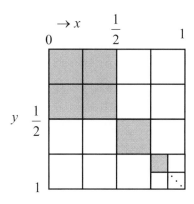

Geometric Probability: Total area is 1, and the area of the shaded region is

$$\left(\frac{1}{2}\right)^2 + \left(\frac{1}{4}\right)^2 + \left(\frac{1}{8}\right)^2 + \left(\frac{1}{16}\right)^2 + \cdots = \left(\frac{1}{2}\right)^2 + \left(\frac{1}{2}\right)^4 + \left(\frac{1}{2}\right)^6 + \left(\frac{1}{2}\right)^8 + \cdots = \frac{\left(\frac{1}{2}\right)^2}{1 - \left(\frac{1}{2}\right)^2} = \frac{1}{3}$$

(Infinite Geometric Series: $\dfrac{a_1}{1-r}$, where $|r| < 1$)

The answer is (D).

3.   First we have to figure out the length of the interval given by $\lfloor x \rfloor = k$ or $k \le x \le k + h$, where $0 \le h < 1$ and $x - k \le h$ In this case, h is the length of the interval.

In this question, if $\lfloor x \rfloor = k$, then $k\left(2014^{x-k} - 1\right) \le 1 \;\rightarrow\; 2014^{x-k} - 1 \le \dfrac{1}{k} \;\rightarrow\; 2014^{x-k} \le 1 + \dfrac{1}{k}$

Now we got $x - k \le \log_{2014}\left(\dfrac{k+1}{k}\right) \;\rightarrow\; x \le k + \log_{2014}\left(\dfrac{k+1}{k}\right)$.

Length of the interval

$$k \qquad\qquad k + \log_{2014}\left(\frac{k+1}{k}\right)$$

Therefore, $\log_{2014}\dfrac{k+1}{k}$ is the length of the interval, where $k = [1, 2013]$.

Now the sum of the intervals is

$$\log_{2014}\left(\frac{2}{1}\right)+\log_{2014}\left(\frac{3}{2}\right)+\log_{2014}\left(\frac{4}{3}\right)+\cdots+\log_{2014}\left(\frac{2014}{2013}\right)=\log_{2014}\left(\frac{\cancel{2}}{1}\cdot\frac{\cancel{3}}{\cancel{2}}\cdot\frac{\cancel{4}}{\cancel{3}}\cdots\frac{2014}{\cancel{2013}}\right)=$$

$$\log_{2014}2014=1.$$

The answer is (A).

4. $\left\lfloor \log 4x \right\rfloor = \left\lfloor \log x \right\rfloor$ and $x \in (0,1)$

We know that $\log x$ have integer values for $x = 1, \dfrac{1}{10}, \dfrac{1}{100}, \dfrac{1}{1000}, \cdots$

For example: $\log 1 = 0, \log \dfrac{1}{10} = -1, \log \dfrac{1}{100} = -2, \cdots$

And also $\log(4x)$ have integers for $x = \dfrac{1}{4}, \dfrac{1}{40}, \dfrac{1}{400}, \cdots$

For example: $\log 4\left(\dfrac{1}{4}\right) = 0, \log 4\left(\dfrac{1}{40}\right) = -1, \log 4\left(\dfrac{1}{400}\right) = -2, \cdots$

		Common Intervals
For $\dfrac{1}{10} \le x < 1$, $\left\lfloor \log x \right\rfloor = -1$	For $\dfrac{1}{40} \le x < \dfrac{1}{4}$, $\left\lfloor \log 4x \right\rfloor = -1$	$\dfrac{1}{10} \le x < \dfrac{1}{4}$
For $\dfrac{1}{100} \le x < \dfrac{1}{10}$, $\left\lfloor \log x \right\rfloor = -2$	For $\dfrac{1}{400} \le x < \dfrac{1}{40}$, $\left\lfloor \log 4x \right\rfloor = -2$	$\dfrac{1}{100} \le x < \dfrac{1}{40}$
For $\dfrac{1}{1000} \le x < \dfrac{1}{100}$, $\left\lfloor \log x \right\rfloor = -3$	For $\dfrac{1}{4000} \le x < \dfrac{1}{400}$, $\left\lfloor \log 4x \right\rfloor = -3$	$\dfrac{1}{1000} \le x < \dfrac{1}{400}$
For $\dfrac{1}{10000} \le x < \dfrac{1}{1000}$, $\left\lfloor \log x \right\rfloor = -4$	For $\dfrac{1}{40000} \le x < \dfrac{1}{4000}$, $\left\lfloor \log 4x \right\rfloor = -4$	$\dfrac{1}{10000} \le x < \dfrac{1}{4000}$
$\vdots$	$\vdots$	$\vdots$

Now find the length of the common intervals.

1) $\dfrac{1}{10} \le x < \dfrac{1}{4}$ $\rightarrow$ $\dfrac{1}{4} - \dfrac{1}{10} = \dfrac{3}{20}$

2) $\dfrac{1}{100} \le x < \dfrac{1}{40}$ $\rightarrow$ $\dfrac{1}{40} - \dfrac{1}{100} = \dfrac{3}{200}$

3) $\dfrac{1}{1000} \le x < \dfrac{1}{400}$ $\rightarrow$ $\dfrac{1}{400} - \dfrac{1}{1000} = \dfrac{3}{2000}$

4) $\dfrac{1}{10000} \le x < \dfrac{1}{4000}$ $\rightarrow$ $\dfrac{1}{4000} - \dfrac{1}{10000} = \dfrac{3}{20000}$

The lengths form a geometric sequence with $r = \dfrac{1}{10}$

Therefore, the probability to choose from the interval $(0,1)$ is

$$P = \frac{3}{20} + \frac{3}{200} + \frac{3}{2000} + \cdots = \frac{\frac{3}{20}}{1 - \frac{1}{10}} = \frac{\frac{3}{20}}{\frac{9}{10}} = \frac{30}{180} = \frac{1}{6}. \quad \left(S = \frac{a_1}{1-r}, |r| < 1 \right)$$

5.   1) $\left\lfloor \sqrt{1} \right\rfloor + \left\lfloor \sqrt{2} \right\rfloor + \left\lfloor \sqrt{3} \right\rfloor = 3$

      2) $\left\lfloor \sqrt{4} \right\rfloor + \left\lfloor \sqrt{5} \right\rfloor + \left\lfloor \sqrt{6} \right\rfloor + \left\lfloor \sqrt{7} \right\rfloor + \left\lfloor \sqrt{8} \right\rfloor = 10$

      3) $\left\lfloor \sqrt{9} \right\rfloor + \left\lfloor \sqrt{10} \right\rfloor + \left\lfloor \sqrt{11} \right\rfloor + \left\lfloor \sqrt{12} \right\rfloor + \left\lfloor \sqrt{13} \right\rfloor + \left\lfloor \sqrt{14} \right\rfloor + \left\lfloor \sqrt{15} \right\rfloor = 21$

      4) $\left\lfloor \sqrt{16} \right\rfloor = 4$

      Therefore, $3 + 10 + 21 + 4 = 38$. The answer is (B).

45	Greatest integer equation (2)

1. We realize $x = 0 \bmod 3$. Now eliminate the floor.

     $\dfrac{x}{3} \le \sqrt{x} < \dfrac{x}{3} + 1 \ \rightarrow \ x \le 3\sqrt{x} < x + 3 \ \rightarrow \ x^2 \le 9x < x^2 + 6x + 9$

     1) $x^2 \le 9x \rightarrow x(x-9) \le 0 \rightarrow x = $ All real numbers

     2) $x^2 + 6x + 9 > 9x \rightarrow x^2 - 3x + 9 > 0 \rightarrow x = $ All real numbers

     From 1) and 2) $\rightarrow 0 \le x \le 9$ and only 0,3,6, and 9 are $0 \bmod 3$.

     The answer is 0,3,6, and 9.

2. Now we know that $n + 1000 \equiv 0 \bmod 70 \ \rightarrow \ n + 20 \bmod 70 \equiv 0 \bmod 70$ and

     $n \equiv 50 \bmod 70$. Now eliminate the floor.

     $\dfrac{n+1000}{70} \le \sqrt{n} < \dfrac{n+1000}{70} + 1 \ \rightarrow \ n + 1000 \le 70\sqrt{n} < n + 1070 \ \rightarrow$

     $n^2 + 2000n + 1000^2 \le 4900n < n^2 + 2140n + 1070^2$

     1) $n^2 + 2000n + 1000^2 \le 4900n \ \rightarrow \ n^2 - 2900n + 1000000 \le 0 \ \rightarrow$

       $(n - 400)(n - 2500) \le 0 \rightarrow 400 \le n \le 2500$

     2) $4900n < n^2 + 2140n + 1070^2 \ \rightarrow \ n^2 - 2760n + 1070^2 > 0 \ \rightarrow$

       $n < 508.5$ or $n > 2251$

       From 1) and 2)

           $400 \le n < 508.5$ or $2251 < n \le 2500$

       In the intervals, only $400, 470, 2290, 2360, 2430, 2500 \equiv 50 \bmod 7$. (Six numbers)

       The answer is (C).

    <u>Easier way:</u>

       Since $n \equiv 50 \bmod 70$, let $n = 70k + 50, (k = 0,1,2,\cdots)$

       When we substitute n with $70k + 50$, we got

       $\dfrac{70k + 1050}{70} = \left\lfloor \sqrt{70k + 50} \right\rfloor \ \rightarrow \ k + 15 = \left\lfloor \sqrt{70k + 50} \right\rfloor$

Now eliminate the floor.

$$k+15 \leq \sqrt{70k+50} < k+16 \rightarrow k^2+30k+225 \leq 70K+50 < k^2+32k+256 \rightarrow$$

1) $k^2+30k+225 \leq 70k+50 \rightarrow (k-5)(k-35) \leq 0$

$$5 \leq k \leq 35$$

2) $70k+50 < k^2+32k+256 \rightarrow k^2-38k-206 > 0$. When we solve,

$$k < 6.6 \text{ or } k > 31.4$$

From 1) and 2) we get

$k = 5,6,32,33,34,35 \rightarrow$ actually $n = 400, 470, 2290, 2360, 2430, 2500 \rightarrow$

6 numbers

3. From $\dfrac{n+5}{7} = \lfloor \sqrt{n} \rfloor$, $n \equiv 2 \bmod 7 \rightarrow n = 7k+2$, $n = 0,1,2,3,\cdots$

Substitute.

$$\frac{7k+7}{7} = \lfloor \sqrt{7k+2} \rfloor \rightarrow k+1 = \sqrt{7k+2} \rightarrow k+1 \leq \sqrt{7k+2} < k+2$$

1) $k+1 \leq \sqrt{7k+2} \rightarrow k^2+2k+1 \leq 7k+2 \rightarrow k^2-5k-1 \leq 0 \rightarrow$

$$-0.22 \leq k \leq 5.2$$

2) $\sqrt{7k+2} < k+2 \rightarrow 7k+2 < k^2+4k+4 \rightarrow k^2-3k+2 > 0 \rightarrow (x-2)(x-1) > 0$

$$k < 1 \text{ or } k > 2$$

From 1) and 2) $-0.22 \leq k < 1$ or $2 < k \leq 5.2$

Therefore, $k = 0,3,4,5 \rightarrow$ Four numbers. The answer is (D).

46	Transformation of a Greatest integer function

1. a) Graph of $y = \lfloor x \rfloor$ b) Graph of $y = \lfloor |x| \rfloor$

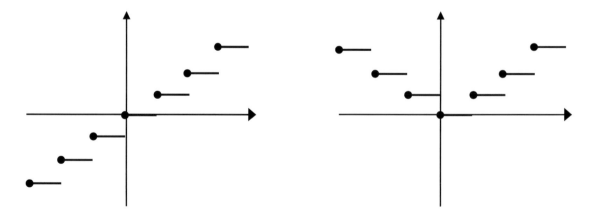

c) Graph of $y = \lfloor -x \rfloor$

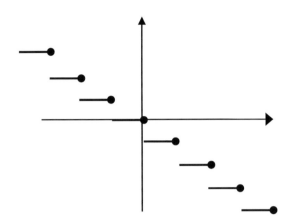

d) Graph of $y = \lfloor -(x-1) \rfloor$

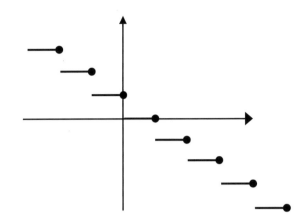

e) Graph of $y = |1 - \lfloor x \rfloor|$

f) Graph of $y = |\lfloor x \rfloor| - |1 - \lfloor x \rfloor|$

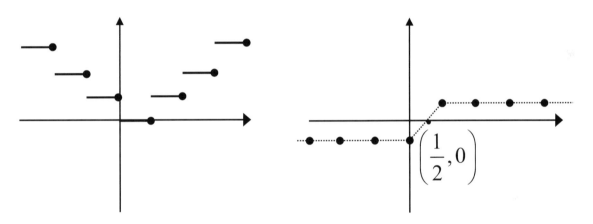

$\left(\dfrac{1}{2}, 0\right)$

The answer is (D).

4 7	General Probability

1. $P(Even) = 3P(odd) \rightarrow P(odd) = \dfrac{1}{4}$ and $P(even) = \dfrac{3}{4}$

   To have even sum of two numbers: $even + even = even$ or $odd + odd = even$.

   Thus, the probability is $P = P(even) \cdot P(even) + P(odd) \cdot P(odd) = \dfrac{3}{4} \times \dfrac{3}{4} + \dfrac{1}{4} \times \dfrac{1}{4} = \dfrac{10}{16} = \dfrac{5}{8}$

   The answer is (E).

2. Expected value $t = \sum_i n_i P_i = 50 \times \dfrac{1}{5} + 20 \times \dfrac{1}{5} + 20 \times \dfrac{1}{5} + 5 \times \dfrac{1}{5} + 5 \times \dfrac{1}{5} = 20$

   Probability to choose a class for a teacher is $P = \dfrac{1}{5}$.

Expected value $s = \sum_i n_i P_i = 50 \times \dfrac{50}{100} + 20 \times \dfrac{20}{100} + 20 \times \dfrac{20}{100} + 5 \times \dfrac{5}{100} + 5 \times \dfrac{5}{100} = 33.5$

Probability to choose a class for a student is

$$P_1 = \frac{50}{100}, P_2 = \frac{20}{100}, P_3 = \frac{20}{100}, P_5 = \frac{5}{100}, P_5 = \frac{5}{100}$$

Therefore, $t - s = 20 - 33.5 = -13.5$. The answer is (B).

3. a) The number of ways to distribute 20 balls into 5 bins : $n_1 = \begin{pmatrix} 20 \\ 3,5,4,4,4 \end{pmatrix}$

$= 5 \times 4 \begin{pmatrix} 20 \\ 3 \end{pmatrix}\begin{pmatrix} 17 \\ 5 \end{pmatrix}\begin{pmatrix} 12 \\ 4 \end{pmatrix}\begin{pmatrix} 8 \\ 4 \end{pmatrix}\begin{pmatrix} 4 \\ 4 \end{pmatrix} = \dfrac{20!}{2!5!4!4!4!}$ into bin 1,2,3,4,5

Remember: Number of ways to arrange in order $= \dfrac{5!}{3!} = 5 \times 4$

a)The number of ways to distribute 20 balls into 5 bins : $n_2 = \begin{pmatrix} 20 \\ 4,4,4,4,4 \end{pmatrix}$

$= \begin{pmatrix} 20 \\ 4 \end{pmatrix}\begin{pmatrix} 20 \\ 4 \end{pmatrix}\begin{pmatrix} 20 \\ 4 \end{pmatrix}\begin{pmatrix} 20 \\ 4 \end{pmatrix}\begin{pmatrix} 20 \\ 4 \end{pmatrix} = \dfrac{20!}{4!4!4!4!4!}$

Remember: Number of ways to arrange in order $= 1$

If total number of arrange the balls into 5 bins is T, then $p = \dfrac{n_1}{T}, q = \dfrac{n_2}{T} \to \dfrac{p}{q} = \dfrac{n_1}{n_2}$

Therefore, $\dfrac{p}{q} = \dfrac{20(20!)}{3!5!4!4!4!} \times \dfrac{4!4!4!4!4!}{20!} = \dfrac{20(4!)(4!)}{3!5!} = 16$

Actually, the value of $T = \begin{pmatrix} 24 \\ 4 \end{pmatrix} = \dfrac{24!}{20!4!}$, see "stars and bars" $n = 20, k = 5$

The answer is (E).

4 8 | Geometric Probability

1. From the figure, the probability that $y > x$ is $\dfrac{1}{8}$. Answer is (A)

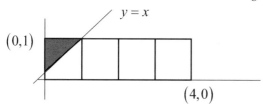

2. Area of the square is 64 and area of the circle is 64π. Therefore, the probability is $\dfrac{256 - 64\pi}{256}$.

The answer is (D).

192

49 | Symmetric Probability (1)

1. We can see there are three different cases, $P(A=B)$, $P(A>B)$, and $P(A<B)$.

   $P(A>B) = P(A<B)$ by symmetric probability and

   $P(A=B) = \dfrac{1}{6} \to (1,1),(2,2),(3,3),(4,4),(5,5),(6,6)$ out of 36 combinations.

   Therefore, $P(A>B) = \dfrac{1-P(A=B)}{2} = \dfrac{1-\dfrac{1}{6}}{2} = \dfrac{5}{12}$. The answer is (B).

2. If Bernard choose three number including 9, then Bernard number is always greater than Silvia's number.

   Bernardo's number   Silvia's number

   $$\{9,\square,\square\} \quad > \quad \{\square,\square,\square\} \; \to \; \text{Probability is } P(\text{contain } 9) = \dfrac{\dbinom{8}{2}}{\dbinom{9}{3}} = \dfrac{1}{3}.$$

   If not, $P(\text{not contain } 9) = \dfrac{2}{3}$. Now we know that $P(B=S) = \dfrac{1}{\dbinom{8}{3}} = \dfrac{1}{56}$

   Therefore, by symmetric probability, $P(B>S) = \dfrac{1}{3} + \dfrac{2}{3}\left(\dfrac{1-\dfrac{1}{56}}{2}\right) = \dfrac{111}{168} = \dfrac{37}{56}$

   The answer is (B).

3. Probability that have the same numbered balls is

   $$P(\text{same numbered bins}) = \left(2^{-1}\right)^2 + \left(2^{-2}\right)^2 + \left(2^{-3}\right)^2 + \cdots = \dfrac{2^{-2}}{1-2^{-2}} = \dfrac{\dfrac{1}{4}}{1-\dfrac{1}{4}} = \dfrac{1}{3}.$$

   Therefore, by the symmetric probability

   $$P(\text{red ball bin number} > \text{green ball bin number}) = \dfrac{1-\dfrac{1}{3}}{2} = \dfrac{1}{3}.$$

4. Probability that players have the same numbers is

   $$P(\text{same numbers}) = \dfrac{1}{\dbinom{10}{2}} = \dfrac{1}{45}$$

   Therefore, by the symmetric probability

$$P(A\text{'s number} < B\text{'s number}) = \frac{1 - \dfrac{1}{45}}{2} = \frac{22}{45}$$

5. The total combinations of picking two books $= \dbinom{10}{2} = 45$.

   For each combination, the number of combinations to have different 3 books is

   $$\begin{cases} \text{Carri 's books:} (B_1, B_2, \square, \square, \square) \\ \text{Betty's books:} (B_1, B_2, \square, \square, \square) \end{cases}$$ the number of choosing different 3 books $= \dbinom{8}{3}\dbinom{5}{3} = 560$.

   Therefore, the probability is

   $$P = \frac{45 \times 560}{\dbinom{10}{5} \times \dbinom{10}{5}} = \frac{45 \times 560}{252 \times 252} = \frac{25}{63}.$$ The answer is (D).

---

5 0	Symmetric Probability (2)

1. By the symmetry of the probability,

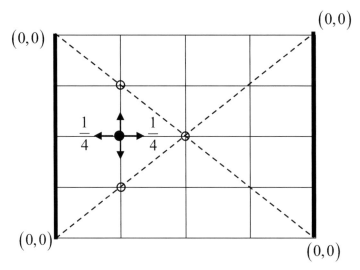

When the point moves to the left, it reached at the vertical side with probability $\dfrac{1}{4}$.

When the point moves up, right, or down, the point lie exactly on the diagonal. At this point, the probability to reach the vertical side is exactly $\dfrac{1}{2}$. Each point has probability $\dfrac{1}{4} \times \dfrac{1}{2} = \dfrac{1}{8}$.

Therefore, total probability is $P = \dfrac{1}{4} + 3\left(\dfrac{1}{8}\right) = \dfrac{5}{8}$. The answer is (B).

1. From the equations, $x + y = 10^z$ and $x^2 + y^2 = 10^{z+1}$, and $x^3 + y^3 = (x+y)(x^2 - xy + y^2)$

   Find $xy : (x+y)^2 = x^2 + 2xy + y^2 \rightarrow (x^2 + y^2) + 2xy = 10^{z+1} + 2xy = 10^{2z}$

   We can have $xy = \dfrac{10^{2z} - 10^{z+1}}{2}$. Now substitute in $x^3 + y^3$

   $x^3 + y^3 = (10^z)\left(10^{z+1} - \left(\dfrac{10^{2z} - 10^{z+1}}{2}\right)\right) = 10^{2z+1} - \left(\dfrac{10^{3z} - 10^{2z+1}}{2}\right) = 10 \cdot 10^{2z} - \dfrac{10^{3z}}{2} + \dfrac{10 \cdot 10^{2z}}{2} =$

   $-\dfrac{1}{2} \cdot 10^{3z} + 15 \cdot 10^{2z}$

   From the expression above, $a = -\dfrac{1}{2}$ and $b = 15$. Therefore, $a + b = -\dfrac{1}{2} + 15 = \dfrac{29}{2}$. Answer is (B).

2. $\log_a b = c^{2005} \rightarrow b = a^{c^{2005}}$

   Case 1) $c = 0$: $b = a^0 = 1 \rightarrow a + b + c = 2005 \rightarrow a + 1 + 0 = 2005 \rightarrow a = 2004$

   Triples are $(2004, 1, 0)$

   Case 2) $c = 1$: $b = a^1 \rightarrow a + b + 1 = 2005 \rightarrow a = 1002, b = 1002, c = 1$

   Triples are $(1002, 1002, 1)$

   Case 3) $c = 2$: $b = a^{2^{2005}} \rightarrow$ Since $a \geq 2$, b must be much greater than 2005.
   We can conclude " If $c = 2, 3, 4, \cdots$, then there is no value of b that satisfies $a + b + c = 2005$.
   It works for only $c = 0$ and $c = 1$. Answer is (C).

3. $a \log_{10} 2 + b \log_{10} 3 + c \log_{10} 5 + d \log_{10} 7 = 2005 \rightarrow \log_{10}\left(2^a \cdot 3^b \cdot 5^c \cdot 7^d\right) = \log_{10} 10^{2005}$

   We can see that $\left(2^a \cdot 3^b \cdot 5^c \cdot 7^d\right) = 10^{2005} = (2 \cdot 5)^{2005} = 2^{2005} \cdot 5^{2005}$

   Therefore, $\left(2^a \cdot 3^b \cdot 5^c \cdot 7^d\right) = 2^{2005} \cdot 3^0 \cdot 5^{2005} \cdot 7^0$ (Prime Factorization)

   Only one four-tuples is available. Answer is (B)

4. $S_1 : \log_{10}\left(1 + x^2 + y^2\right) \leq \log_{10} 10 + \log_{10}(x+y) \rightarrow 1 + x^2 + y^2 \leq 10x + 10y$

   $x^2 - 10x + y^2 - 10y \leq -1 \rightarrow (x-5)^2 + (y-5)^2 \leq 49 \rightarrow$ Circle with $r^2 = 49$.

   $S_2 : \log_{10}\left(2 + x^2 + y^2\right) \leq \log_{10} 100 + \log_{10}(x+y) \rightarrow 2 + x^2 + y^2 \leq 100x + 100y$

   $x^2 - 100x + y^2 - 100y \leq -2 \rightarrow (x-50)^2 + (y-50)^2 \leq -2 + 2500 + 2500$

   $(x-50)^2 + (y-50)^2 \leq 4998 \rightarrow$ Circle with $r^2 = 4998$.

   Area of circle 1 is 49π, and area of circle 2 is 4998π.

   Therefore, $\dfrac{S_2}{S_1} = \dfrac{4998\pi}{49\pi} = 102$. Answer is (E).

5. We can see: $r = \log_{10}(a^2) \rightarrow r = 2\log_{10} a \rightarrow \log a = \dfrac{r}{2}$ and

$$2\pi r = \log_{10}(b^4) \rightarrow 2\pi r = 4\log_{10} b \rightarrow \log_{10} b = \dfrac{2\pi r}{4} = \dfrac{\pi r}{2}$$

Therefore, $\log_a b = \dfrac{\log b}{\log a} = \dfrac{\pi r/2}{r/2} = \pi$. Answer is (C).

6. We know that $\log_{\sqrt{2}} \sqrt{x} = \log_2 x = \log_4 x^2 = \log_8 x^3 = \log_{16} x^4$.

So $5\log_2 x = 40$. $\log_2 x = 8 \rightarrow x = 2^8 = 256$ Answer is (D).

---

5 2	Factoring $x^{2n+1} - 1$, $x^{2n+1} + 1$

1. To solve this type of question, we need a skill.

Let $x = 2^{17}$. Then we got $\dfrac{x^{17}+1}{x+1}$.

We know that $x^{17} + 1 = (x+1)\left(x^{16} - x^{15} + x^{14} - x^{13} + x^{12} - \cdots + x^2 - x + 1\right)$.

So, $\dfrac{x^{17}+1}{x+1} = \left(x^{16} - x^{15} + x^{14} - x^{13} + x^{12} - \cdots + x^2 - x + 1\right)$. But this is not an increasing sequence.

Change the form in positive number as follows.

$$\left(x^{16} - x^{15}\right) + \left(x^{14} - x^{13}\right) + x^{12} - \cdots + \left(x^2 - x\right) + 1$$

One more time factoring

$$x^{15}(x-1) + x^{13}(x-1) + x^{11}(x-1) + \cdots x(x-1) + 1 \rightarrow$$
$$(x-1)\left(x^{15} + x^{13} + x^{11} + \cdots + x\right) + 1$$

But still we don't get an increasing sequence, because of $(x-1)$.

$x - 1 = 2^{17} - 1$

Consider this number: Let $2^{17} - 1 = y^{17} - 1$.

$y^{17} - 1 = (y-1)\left(y^{16} + y^{15} + y^{14} + \cdots + y + 1\right)$

If $y = 2$, then

$2^{17} - 1 = 2^{16} + 2^{15} + 2^{14} + 2^{13} + \cdots 2^1 + 1$

Actually, there are 17 terms in $(x-1)$ and 8 terms in $\left(x^{15} + x^{13} + x^{11} + \cdots + x\right)$.

Therefore, total terms will be generated from $17 \times 8 + 1 = 137$ as follows.

$$\underbrace{(x-1)}_{17\,\text{terms}}\underbrace{\left(x^{15} + x^{13} + x^{11} + \cdots + x\right)}_{8\,\text{terms}} + \underbrace{1}_{1\,\text{term}}$$

The answer is (C).

2. $10^{1002} - 4^{501} = 2^{1002} \cdot 5^{1002} - 2^{1002} = 2^{1002}\left(5^{1002} - 1\right)$

Now, $5^{1002} - 1 = \left(5^{501} - 1\right)\left(5^{501} + 1\right)$.

We know that $5^{501}-1=(5-1)(5^{500}+5^{499}+\cdots+1)$ and $5^{501}+1=(5+1)\left(5^{500}-5^{499}+5^{496}-\cdots+1\right)$

Therefore, $5^{1002}-1=\left(5^{501}-1\right)\left(5^{501}+1\right)=24(5^{500}+5^{499}+\cdots+1)(5^{500}-5^{499}+\cdots+1)$.

Ans also $(5^{500}+5^{499}+\cdots+5^{1}+1)\equiv 1(\bmod 2)$ and $\left(5^{500}-5^{499}+5^{496}-\cdots-5^{1}+1\right)\equiv 1(\bmod 2)$,

Which are all odd. Now $24=2^{3}\times 3$. Now we can see
$$10^{1002}-4^{501}=2^{1002}\cdot 2^{5}\cdot\left(5^{500}-5^{499}+\cdots\right)\left(5^{500}+500^{499}+\cdots\right)$$

Therefore, the greatest power of 2 is $2^{1002}\cdot 2^{3}=3^{1005}$.
The answer is (D)

53	Express a number as sum of consecutive positive numbers

1. a) $k=$ odd and the median $=m \rightarrow mk=65=5\times 13$

m	k	Representations
13	5	$11+12+\boxed{13}+14+15$
5	13	Negative terms

There is only one way.

b) $k=$ even and the median $\dfrac{2m+1}{2}$ $\rightarrow \dfrac{(2m+1)k}{2}=65 \rightarrow (2m+1)k=130=2\times 5\times 13$

$2m+1$	$k=$ even	Representations
65 $m=32$, $m+1=33$	2	$32+33$
13 $m=6, m=7$	10	$2+3+4+5+6+7+8+9+10+11$

Two ways

Therefore, there are three ways to express the number.

2. a) $k=$ odd and the median $=m \rightarrow mk=2012=2\times 2\times 503$

m	k	Representations
4	503	Negative terms

b) $k = $ even and the median $\dfrac{2m+1}{2}$

$$\rightarrow \dfrac{(2m+1)k}{2} = 2012 \rightarrow (2m+1)k = 4024 = 2\times 2\times 2\times 503$$

$2m+1$	$k = $ even	Representations
503 $m = 251$, $m+1 = 252$	8	248+249+250+251+252+253+254+255

The smallest of these integers is 248.

3. a) $k = $ odd and the median $= m \quad \rightarrow mk = 345 = 3\times 5\times 23$

m	k	Representations
115	3	114+115+116
69	5	67+68+69+70+71
15	23	4+5+$\cdots$ +15+$\cdots$ +26
5	69	Negative terms

3 ways

b) $k = $ even and the median $\dfrac{2m+1}{2} \quad \rightarrow \dfrac{(2m+1)k}{2} = 345 \rightarrow (2m+1)k = 690 = 2\times 3\times 5\times 23$

$2m+1$	$k = $ even	Representations
345 $m = 172$, $m+1 = 173$	2	172+173
115 $m = 57$, $m+1 = 58$	6	55+56+57+58+589+60
69 $m = 34$, $m+1 = 35$	10	30+31+32+33+34+35+36+37+38+39
23 $m = 11$, $m+1 = 12$	30	Negative terms

4 ways

Therefore, there is 7 ways to express 345 as a sum of positive consecutive integers.

4. a) $k =$ odd and the median $= m \rightarrow mk = 483 = 3 \times 7 \times 23$

m	k	Representations
161	3	160+161+162
69	7	66+67+68+69+70+71+72
21	23	10+11+12+$\cdots$ +21+$\cdots$ +31+32

b) $k =$ even and the median $\dfrac{2m+1}{2} \rightarrow \dfrac{(2m+1)k}{2} = 483 \rightarrow (2m+1)k = 966 = 2 \times 3 \times 7 \times 23$

$2m+1$	$k =$ even	Representations
23 $m = 11$, $m+1 = 12$	42	Negative terms
69 $m = 34$, $m+1 = 35$	14	28+29+$\cdots$ +34+35+$\cdots$ +40+41

Therefore, when we express as a sum of 23 consecutive integers, the smallest is 10. Answer is (D).

54   Abraham de Moivre's Formula

1. a) $2 - 2i = 2\sqrt{2}\left(\dfrac{1}{\sqrt{2}} - \dfrac{1}{\sqrt{2}}i \right) = 2\sqrt{2}\left(\cos\dfrac{7\pi}{4} + i\sin\dfrac{7\pi}{4} \right)$

b) $-6i = 6\left(\cos\dfrac{3\pi}{2} + i\sin\dfrac{3\pi}{2} \right)$

c) $-1 + i = \sqrt{2}\left(\cos\dfrac{3\pi}{4} + i\sin\dfrac{3\pi}{4} \right)$

2. a) $6cis120° = 6(\cos 120 + i\sin 120) = 6\left(-\frac{1}{2} + i\frac{\sqrt{3}}{2}\right) = -3 + 3\sqrt{3}\,i$

b) $e^{i\frac{\pi}{3}} = \cos\frac{\pi}{3} + i\sin\frac{\pi}{3} = \frac{1}{2} + \frac{\sqrt{3}}{2}i$

c) $9cis\frac{3\pi}{4} = 9\left(\cos\frac{3\pi}{4} + i\sin\frac{3\pi}{4}\right) = 9\left(-\frac{1}{2} + \frac{\sqrt{3}}{2}i\right) = -\frac{9}{2} + \frac{9\sqrt{3}}{2}i$

3. a) $1 - i = \sqrt{2}\left(\cos\frac{7\pi}{4} + i\sin\frac{7\pi}{4}\right) = \sqrt{2}e^{i\frac{7\pi}{4}}$

b) $\frac{1}{2} - \frac{\sqrt{3}}{2}i = e^{i\frac{5\pi}{3}}$

c) $-3i = 3e^{i\frac{3\pi}{2}}$

4. Let $z = a + bi$ and $\bar{z} = a - bi$. $|z| = \sqrt{a^2 + b^2}$

$z \cdot \bar{z} = (a + bi)(a - bi) = a^2 + b^2 = |z|^2$

5. $\theta_1 = \tan^{-1}\frac{1}{3} \;\rightarrow\; z_1 = 3 + i = \sqrt{10}\left(\cos\theta_1 + i\sin\theta_1\right)$

$\theta_2 = \tan^{-1}\frac{1}{4} \;\rightarrow\; z_2 = 4 + i = \sqrt{17}\left(\cos\theta_2 + i\sin\theta_2\right)$

$\theta_3 = \tan^{-1}\frac{1}{5} \;\rightarrow\; z_3 = 5 + i = \sqrt{26}\left(\cos\theta_3 + i\sin\theta_3\right)$

$\theta_4 = \tan^{-1}\frac{1}{n} \;\rightarrow\; z_4 = n + i = \sqrt{n^2 + 1}\left(\cos\theta_4 + i\sin\theta_4\right)$

Now, $z_1 z_2 z_3 z_4 = \left(\sqrt{10}\right)\left(\sqrt{17}\right)\left(\sqrt{26}\right)\left(\sqrt{n^2 + 1}\right)\left[\cos\left(\theta_1 + \theta_2 + \theta_3 + \theta_4\right) + i\sin\left(\theta_1 + \theta_2 + \theta_3 + \theta_4\right)\right]$

And $\tan^{-1}\frac{1}{3} + \tan^{-1}\frac{1}{4} + \tan^{-1}\frac{1}{5} + \tan^{-1}\frac{1}{n} = \theta_1 + \theta_2 + \theta_3 + \theta_4 = \frac{\pi}{4}$

Therefore, $(3 + i)(4 + i)(5 + i)(n + i) = \left(\sqrt{10}\right)\left(\sqrt{17}\right)\left(\sqrt{26}\right)\left(\sqrt{n^2 + 1}\right)\left[\cos\left(\frac{\pi}{4}\right) + i\sin\left(\frac{\pi}{4}\right)\right]$

$\rightarrow (48n - 46) + i(48 + 46n) = \left(\sqrt{10}\right)\left(\sqrt{17}\right)\left(\sqrt{26}\right)\left(\sqrt{n^2 + 1}\right)\left[\cos\left(\frac{\pi}{4}\right) + i\sin\left(\frac{\pi}{4}\right)\right]$

Thus, $\tan \theta = \left(\dfrac{48+46n}{48n-46}\right) = \tan \dfrac{\pi}{4} = 1$

Solve for n.

$$\left(\dfrac{48+46n}{48n-46}\right) = 1 \;\rightarrow\; 48+46n = 48n-46 \;\rightarrow\; 2n=94 \;\rightarrow\; n=47$$

Answer is $n=47$.

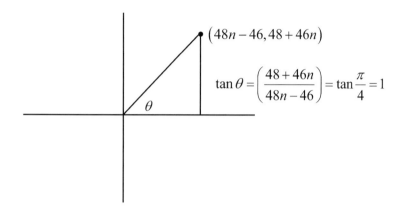

55	Roots of $f(x)=x^n-1$

1. $f(x)=(x-1)\left(x^8+x^7+x^6+x^5+x^4+x^3+x^2+x+1\right)=x^9-1$

   Angle between roots is $\dfrac{2\pi}{9}$.

   The roots of $f(x)=0$ are $1, e^{i\frac{2\pi}{9}}, e^{i\frac{4\pi}{9}}, e^{i\frac{6\pi}{9}}, e^{i\frac{8\pi}{9}}, e^{i\frac{10\pi}{9}}, e^{i\frac{12\pi}{9}}, e^{i\frac{14\pi}{9}}, e^{i\frac{16\pi}{9}}$.

   Except $x=1$, the roots are $e^{i\frac{2\pi}{9}}, e^{i\frac{4\pi}{9}}, e^{i\frac{6\pi}{9}}, e^{i\frac{8\pi}{9}}, e^{i\frac{10\pi}{9}}, e^{i\frac{12\pi}{9}}, e^{i\frac{14\pi}{9}}, e^{i\frac{16\pi}{9}}$.

2. $f(x)=\left(x^2-1\right)\left(x^6+x^4+x^2+1\right)=x^8-1$

   Let $X=x^2$. Then, $f(X)=(X-1)\left(X^3+X^2+X+1\right)=X^4-1$

   Angle between the roots is $\dfrac{2\pi}{4}=\dfrac{\pi}{2}$.

   The roots are $X=1, e^{i\frac{\pi}{2}}, e^{i\pi}, e^{i\frac{3\pi}{2}} \;\rightarrow\; x=\pm1, \left(\pm e^{i\frac{\pi}{2}}\right)^{\frac{1}{2}}, \left(\pm e^{i\pi}\right)^{\frac{1}{2}}, \left(\pm e^{i\frac{3\pi}{2}}\right)^{\frac{1}{2}}$

   Remember: $-e^{i\frac{\pi}{4}}=e^{i\frac{5\pi}{4}}$, $-e^{i\frac{\pi}{2}}=e^{i\frac{3\pi}{2}}$, $-e^{i\frac{3\pi}{4}}=e^{i\frac{7\pi}{4}}$

   Therefore, the roots of the equation (except $1,-1$) are

   $$e^{i\frac{\pi}{4}}, e^{i\frac{\pi}{2}}, e^{i\frac{3\pi}{4}}, e^{i\frac{5\pi}{4}}, e^{i\frac{3\pi}{2}}, e^{i\frac{7\pi}{4}}.$$

Made in United States
Troutdale, OR
09/22/2024

23031691R00113